KING ARTHUR

Christopher Hibbert

HORIZON · NEW WORD CITY

Published by New Word City, Inc.

For more information about New Word City, visit our Web site at
NewWordCity.com

American Heritage Publishing
Edwin S. Grosvenor, President
P.O. Box 1488
Rockville, MD 20851

1
THE TRUTH IN THE LEGEND   5

2
LE MORTE D'ARTHUR   25

3
THE LIFE OF ARTHUR   45

4
CENTURY OF CONFLICT   53

5
ARTHUR AT WAR   71

6
UNEARTHING CAMELOT   97

7
UNMISTAKABLE TRUTHS   111

8
LOVE, LEGEND, AND LEGACY   133

1
THE TRUTH IN THE LEGEND

In the heart of the quiet countryside of southwest England, a yellow limestone hill rises sharply above the village of South Cadbury. Old men who have lived all their lives in its shadow have strange tales to tell. It's a hollow hill, they believe, and if, on St. John's Eve, the summer solstice, you could find the golden gates that lead inside, you would discover King Arthur holding court. Sometimes, they say, on stormy winter nights, you can hear the king trot by along the well-worn track. As one man put it, "Folks do say that on the night of the full moon King Arthur and his men ride round the hill, and their horses are shod with silver and a silver shoe has been found in the track where they do ride, and when they have ridden round the hill, they stop to water their horses at the Wishing Well."

For generations, such legends have been told of Arthur, the Once and Future King, and his knights at South Cadbury, which has long been identified with Arthur's home of Camelot, but also across England, Wales, and Scotland.

Each county has its legends. In Cornwall, the tale goes that all the farmlands and the forests "swarmed with giants until Arthur, the good king, vanished them all with his cross-sword." In Northumberland, beneath the castle of Sewingshields, Arthur and his queen, Guinevere, their knights and ladies, and the king's hounds lie sleeping in the vaults. So, too, do they rest beneath the ruins of Richmond Castle in Yorkshire, waiting to be awakened by the blast of a horn that lies on a table by the entrance to their cavern. An unwary farmer once stumbled upon them, it is said, but lacked the courage to blow the horn that would bring them back to life. Wales is full of tales of caves and hollow hills in which Arthur and his knights await the call to return. One day, these legends agree, Arthur will be roused from his slumber and ride forth to save his people, at a time when they most need him.

As well as legends, there are places Arthur is said to have traveled. His name can be found the length and breadth of the country - from the Scilly islands of Great and Little Arthur off the southwestern coast of Cornwall, to Arthur's Seat, looming above Scotland's capital city of Edinburgh, far to the north; and from Arthur's Chair in the hills of Breconshire in Wales to Arthur's Hill at Newcastle, on the northeastern coast of Northumberland. No other name in Britain turns up so frequently except that of the Devil. No one knows exactly how old these place names are, just as no one knows how old the legends are. But somewhere in the mists of history, there was a real Arthur who inspired them.

The Arthur who has become part of our imagination today is mostly a creation of medieval times, when troubadours and chroniclers made him into a romantic hero, a Christian champion, a noble ruler whose knights were models of chivalry. These Arthurian tales have taken their place in our literature, and over the centuries, poets and painters have recreated the characters and their adventures many times over. The myth has become so real that most people forget the existence of a historical Arthur. He may not have been a king or even a particularly good or idealistic man. Yet, despite the vague historical record, he must have been a remarkable person because fame does not come without merit, and Arthur's fame seldom has been equaled.

The earliest known reference to Arthur dates from the turbulent centuries immediately after 410 A.D., when the last Roman garrison was withdrawn from Britain, then the westernmost outpost of the crumbling Roman Empire. Following the legions' departure, the island suffered constant invasions by Jutes, Angles, and Saxons from across the North Sea. In an epic poem written circa 603, the Welsh bard Aneurin describes one of the many desperate battles that took place between these invaders and the Britons. From this long poem, Y Gododdin, Arthur's name already was identified with outstanding courage, for Aneurin describes the feats of a British hero by saying that his valor was remarkable, "although he was no Arthur."

It's also significant that a century before Y Gododdin was written, the name Arthur virtually was unknown in Britain. By the late sixth and early seventh centuries, however, there are four or five Arthurs in the scanty records that have survived from this period. One of them was a prince of Argyll born to the Scottish king Aedán mac Gabráin about 570. Another Arthur entered the world at much the same time in southwestern Wales, great-grandson of a ruler named Vortiporius, while in 620 the Irish king Morgan was killed by one "Artuir, son of Bicoir, a Briton." It is difficult to account for this sudden popularity of the name unless a real Arthur existed whose exploits had so excited his contemporaries that several British leaders named their sons in his honor.

Although these references suggest that a historical Arthur was living in Britain sometime during the sixth century, the sources do not mention his name directly. It is not until some 250 years later that Arthur's name first appears in the *Historia Brittonum*, compiled in Latin by a Welsh monk named Nennius in the ninth century. In tantalizingly brief references, Nennius mentions Arthur as the British victor in a series of sixth-century battles fought by the Britons against the Saxons. Nennius gives little reliable information, but he does confirm Arthur's legendary reputation for bravery and makes clear that Arthur was a figure around whom fantastic legends already had begun to cluster.

Nennius recounts two stories that illustrate this; he calls them mirabilia - marvels. The first concerns Carn Cavall, a cairn, or monument, made from stones piled on top of each other, in the Welsh county of Breconshire. On the top of the cairn was a stone bearing the footprint of Arthur's dog, Cavall, who had marked it by treading on it during a boar hunt. Arthur had built the cairn as a memorial to his beloved dog; whenever the stone with the footprint was removed, within twenty-four hours, it would be back on its heap.

The other story was of the miraculous tomb of Arthur's son Anir, who was buried beside the River Gamber in Herefordshire on the Welsh border. Anir "was the son of Arthur the soldier," Nennius writes, "and Arthur himself killed him there and buried him. And when men come to measure the length of the mound, they find it sometimes six feet, sometimes nine, sometimes twelve, and sometimes fifteen. Whatever length you find it at one time, you will find it different at another, and I . . . have proved this to be true."

Fanciful as Nennius' stories appear, they were outdone by a twelfth-century scholar known as Geoffrey of Monmouth. In his book, *Historia Regum Britanniae (A History of the Kings of Britain)*, he provided an account of "the kings who dwelt in Britain before the coming of Christ," and "especially of King Arthur and the many others who succeeded him after the coming of Christ." Geoffrey probably was born in South Wales, although he may originally have been of Breton stock. All we know for certain is that his father was called Arthur and that he ended his life as bishop of St. Asaph, a town in North Wales. Geoffrey, an imaginative man who was proud of his Celtic origins, also was a well-read and ambitious man who shared the heritage of the Normans, the overlords of Britain at the time. His *History of the Kings of Britain* presents the Arthurian legend in a way that appealed to a far wider audience than the Norman noblemen to whom it was dedicated.

History is divided into twelve books, three of which are devoted to Arthur, and it is clear that he excites the author's imagination more than all the other British kings. Here, Arthur appears as the great romantic hero of the Celtic tradition. He has a magical sword, shield painted with the likeness of the Blessed Mary, Mother of God, spear "thirsty for slaughter," and helmet whose crest is "carved in the shape of a dragon." His court is described as magnificent as that of the Emperor Charlemagne, and its atmosphere is pervaded with twelfth-century chivalric ideals: "For none was thought worthy of a lady's love, unless he had been three times approved in the bearing of arms. And so the ladies were made chaste and the knights the better by their loves."

In Geoffrey's *History of the Kings of Britain*, the traditions and stories of the Arthurian epic are established for the first time. Here, too, is the first suggestion that Arthur did not merely defeat the Saxons. He led British armies overseas on triumphant campaigns that ranged from Ireland to the borders of Italy, bringing them victories worthy of those won by Caesar.

According to Geoffrey, his vivid - or as many were to say, incredible - narrative was based upon "a very ancient book in the British tongue." It was brought to England from Wales by his friend Walter, Archdeacon of Oxford, "a man well informed about the history of foreign countries, and most learned in all branches of history." Because no one other than Geoffrey and Walter appears ever to have seen this old book, and no Welsh or Breton chronicle that resembles it ever has been discovered, it long has been supposed that Geoffrey just invented it. It was customary in those days, when compiling a history whose accuracy might be questioned, to claim that its authority was vouched for by a work of antiquity. In any case, Geoffrey of Monmouth ended his book with a note that he has left the retelling of the biographies of the later Welsh and Saxon kings to three other contemporary historians. Perhaps he expected them to be his critics as well, because he recommends that they "say nothing at all about the kings of the Britons, since they have not in their possession the book in the British language which Walter, Archdeacon of Oxford, brought from Wales. It is this book which I have been at such pains to translate thus into Latin, for it was composed very accurately about the deeds of these princes and to their honor."

One historian undeterred by this warning was William of Newburgh, who was born about 1136, the year Geoffrey finished his *History*, and who subsequently wrote a history of English affairs from the Norman Conquest onward. A far more critical historian than Geoffrey, William strongly condemned his predecessor's work, remarking that if the events it related ever happened, they must have taken place in a different world. Geoffrey, according to William, had made "the little finger of his Arthur thicker than the loins of Alexander the Great."

Later historians agreed with early skeptics in disbelieving the tale that the ancient book had been found by the Archdeacon of Oxford and argued Geoffrey made up his stories. Geoffrey's *History* appeared during the troubled reign of King Stephen, when the Norman dynasty ruling England was in danger of losing its power and influence and its members felt the need for a glorious predecessor on the throne. Charlemagne was already an accepted folk hero who, legend said, was not dead, but only sleeping, waiting to return in triumph with his paladins. A relationship with the legendary Arthur could greatly benefit the Norman kings in their efforts to throw off French domination.

Other historians have stressed that Geoffrey was brought up in the atmosphere of Celtic lore. While complimenting the royal court by presenting Arthur as the ideal Anglo-Norman king, he also was flattering the Celts by exaggerating the splendors of their past. In truth, he was not writing history at all, but recounting the stupendous victories of the British over their enemies.

Yet Geoffrey of Monmouth's place in this story is important, for it was he who created the Arthurian legend that fired the imagination of the Christian world. His popularity can be judged from the fact that nearly 200 of his manuscripts have survived, some dating from the twelfth century. Throughout the Middle Ages, Geoffrey's *History* remained the primary source for all writers about Celtic Britain.

On the Continent, the legend of Arthur was expanded and embellished. As early as the 1140s, Geoffrey Gaimar had translated Geoffrey's *History* from Latin into French. In 1155, the Anglo-Norman poet Maistre Wace brought out a verse paraphrase, "Le Roman de Brut," introducing the legend of the Round Table. He presented Arthur as "a lover of glory, whose famous deeds are right fit to be kept in remembrance: He ordained the courtesies of courts, and observed high state in a very splendid fashion."

Around 1175, the Arthurian legend was taken up by the French poet Chrétien de Troyes, who, in response to the wishes of his patroness, Countess Marie de Champagne, added fresh characters and a fresh flavor to the stories, casting the tales in an ethereal setting in which love was a kind of religion. This type of ritualized behavior glorified the affection between a knight and his lady - who could not be his wife, since all marriages were arranged, and true love within such a relationship was almost out of the question. Courtly love dictated that the lover should be humble and courteous, and revere and obey his lady as if she were his lord; in return, the lady would reward his devotion by loving him as completely as she pleased. Understandably, the ideals of courtly love became popular, and the stories that glorified it were read and recited all over Europe.

Following Chrétien's example, several other French writers produced prose and verse romances, and began grouping them together. Storytellers from Brittany added to the increasing body of material with their detailed accounts of Arthurian adventures based on old Celtic tales of marvels and magic, which they retold as they wandered from one nobleman's hall to the next.

In England, a Worcestershire priest named Layamon translated Wace's "Roman de Brut" from French into English, again expanding and elaborating the basic material. In Layamon's Brut, the emphasis changes once more: Layamon was writing not for the aristocracy, but for the common people of England, who mainly were interested in the characters and adventures already familiar to them from their native heritage. Layamon treats the legend as an epic of early Britain in which Arthur is a practical, nationalistic, somewhat barbaric leader, very different from the magical fairy king of the French romances. This earthier, straightforward Arthur is an essentially British hero, and this treatment of him is continued in several later English poems and romances that retell the adventures of the king and his knights.

The first appearance of King Arthur in a work of art was not in his native realm of Britain, but in Italy, where a relief of Arthur and his knights was carved above the north doorway of the Modena Cathedral sometime between 1099 and 1120. In 1165, Arthur was again depicted, this time on a mosaic pavement in the cathedral of Otranto, on the southern heel of Italy. The mosaic portrays the king bearing a scepter and riding a goat, which seems an odd mount for a king - except that goats at that time had some association with those who, like Arthur, supposedly ruled subterranean kingdoms.

About thirty years after this mosaic was laid down, an English visitor to the island of Sicily, not far distant, reported that its inhabitants believed Arthur could be found in the volcanic depths below Mt. Etna. He had also been seen on a Sicilian plain by a groom in search of a runaway horse. This man had crossed the plain, entered an ornate palace, and found King Arthur lying on a bed. The king told him of his last battle and that each year, on the anniversary of that battle, his wounds broke out afresh. It is surprising that the tradition of Arthur's survival traveled so far from its British origins, but the island of Sicily was ruled at this time by a Norman dynasty. The legend well could have been imported by storytellers in their service and transplanted into a Mediterranean setting by their eager listeners.

Within two centuries, the legend of King Arthur and his knights spread across Europe and into parts of Asia. In France, Arthur's fame almost eclipsed that of Charlemagne, who was not restored to his preeminence until the Middle Ages had drawn to a close. In Germany, medieval poets celebrated Arthur's deeds and the adventures of his knights, particularly Tristan and Percival. In Italy, Dante wrote of Lancelot. Translations of Arthurian texts made their way from Ireland to Greece; his name was familiar throughout the Low Countries and in Scandinavia and Switzerland, Spain and Portugal, Cyprus and Sicily.

"Whither has not flying fame spread the name of Arthur the Briton?" asked an English writer as early as the 1170s. "Even as far as the empire of Christendom extends. Who, I say, does not speak of Arthur the Briton, since he is almost better known to the people of Asia than to the Britanni, as our pilgrims returning from the East inform us. The Eastern people speak of him, as do the Western, though separated by the width of the whole earth."

Early in the thirteenth century, noblemen and knights began festivities that came to be called Round Tables, in honor of the great table around which Arthur's knights sat at Camelot. The idea of a round table that made no distinction between the ranks of the knights who sat at it seemed to appeal to the medieval mind - no doubt in contrast to the rules of precedence that governed every other activity, especially eating in company. Crusaders who battled to free the Holy Land from Moslem domination also entertained themselves with jousts and banquets that honored the legendary Arthur; the Lord of Beirut honored the knighting of his eldest sons with a celebration at which "there was much giving and spending; there were bohorts [a tournament at which blunted weapons were used], the adventures of Britain and the Round Table were enacted, and there were many other amusements."

Similar Round Table festivities are reported from places as diverse as Cyprus in 1223, Acre in 1286, Valencia in 1269, Prague in 1319, and as far west as Dublin in 1498. Here and many other places, kings, dukes, and emperors founded orders in imitation of King Arthur's "goodly fellowship." They, their knights, guests, and rivals adopted the names, supposed heraldic badges, splendid clothes, and outfits of Arthur's famous knights and competed in energetic and dangerous tournaments for the pleasure and favors of the ladies of the court.

Popes condemned the immorality and wantonness of the Round Tables; those who died after a heavy fall or ferocious blow were denied Christian burial. But the Round Table continued to be the most fashionable diversion among European nobility.

Although primarily associated with the aristocracy, the Round Table was not an exclusively upper-class activity. In 1281, a citizen of Magdeburg in Saxony sent invitations to various acquaintances, asking them to attend a Round Table and compete in a tournament, the prize to be a woman named Dame Feie. Those who came to demonstrate their skill were met by constables outside the city and escorted to the tourney grounds. The shields of the defending champions were hung from trees, and a touch with a lance on one would bring its owner out from his tent nearby to meet the challenger and defend his honor. Dame Feie was, indeed, won - by an old merchant who presented her with a considerable dowry - but it is hard to believe that he won her by force of arms alone.

One of the most magnificent of all medieval tournaments was held at Windsor Castle in 1344 by Edward III, who ordered it to celebrate two resounding victories against England's traditional enemies, France and Scotland. After three days of jousting and feasting, the king assembled his guests. Dressed in velvet robes and wearing the crown of England, he placed his hand on the Bible and "took a corporeal oath that he would begin a Round Table in the same manner and condition as the Lord Arthur, formerly King of England, appointed it, namely to the number of 300 knights . . . and he would cherish it and maintain it according to his power." Edward selected his knights, binding them to himself, to each other, and to the service of the weak and oppressed, with solemn oaths; then, says the chronicler, the kettledrums and trumpets sounded "all together, and the guests hastened to a feast; which feast was complete with richness of fare, variety of dishes, and overflowing abundance of drinks; the delight was unutterable, the comfort inestimable, the enjoyment unalloyed, the hilarity without care."

Several days later, in the courtyard of the castle's Upper Ward, work began on a great stone hall for the Round Table, where the knights of the fellowship could hold their feasts. Soon afterward, it had to be suspended, for the king went to war with France once more and could not afford the double expense. He returned to Windsor in 1347, triumphant after his crushing victory over the French at Crécy and his capture of the port of Calais, the key to the English Channel. The unfinished hall for the knights of the Round Table still stood in the Upper Ward to remind him of his intentions. Edward, a man of great ambition, took his obligations as a knight and as a leader of knights more seriously than his responsibility as sovereign. He soon was considering an enterprise "more particular and more select," the revival of his idea for a fellowship of knights that would be the envy of Europe.

So it was that the Round Table of King Arthur became the original inspiration of the Order of the Garter. This order, which took its name from the badges worn by the knights who competed in a tournament held at Windsor in 1348, was to become, and still remains, in the twenty-first century, the most noble and respected order of knighthood in Europe.

By the time the order was founded, however, the ideals of chivalry were dying. Battles no longer were won by brave knights fighting each other with sword and lance. Edward III's victory at Crécy had proved that a quantity of low-born English longbowmen, posted advantageously, could gain a victory over a knightly army twice the size, despite its superior armor and aristocratic birth. At Agincourt in northern France in 1415, the lesson was underscored when a French army of 50,000 clashed with an English force of 13,000. Thousands of French knights, the glory of the chivalry of King Charles VI, refused to allow what they perceived as inferior troops and the new, despised artillery a place in the front line. Dismounted, in a dense metal wedge, unable to move in the muddy fields, they were at the mercy of the English archers and men-at-arms. The Englishmen, free to maneuver, simply pushed the French knights to the ground in their heavy armor and dispatched them with their own swords and battle-axes.

Within another half-century, England was to be torn asunder by civil war as the brutal Wars of the Roses convulsed the country. The Middle Ages were drawing to a close; new ideas, new ways of life, new inventions were being introduced. In

1476, William Caxton set up the first printing press in England and began to print books that previously had been available only in laboriously copied manuscript: Chaucer's *Canterbury Tales*, translations from the classics, an encyclopedia of philosophy.

On July 31, 1485, Caxton published his sixty-second title from the sign of the Red Pale in the London parish of Westminster. Within a month, the first Tudor king of England would ascend the throne; a new era was about to begin. The book Caxton printed that July, though, was the most renowned of all medieval romances, Sir Thomas Malory's *Le Morte d'Arthur* - a book that looked back to the glories and heroic achievements of a more chivalrous age, already forgotten and idealized.

2
LE MORTE D'ARTHUR

Caxton called it a "noble and joyous book," but *Le Morte d'Arthur* is also full of a sense of doom that foreshadows the "dolorous death and departing out of this world" of its great hero and his valiant knights. Its author was a prisoner when he wrote it, a prisoner who longed for the day of his deliverance. He was probably Sir Thomas Malory, a Warwickshire gentleman who once served in Parliament. Later, however, he apparently turned to a life of crime. Accusations of rape, robbery, cattle thieving, extortion, and attempted murder are recorded against him, and he was imprisoned for years in Newgate Prison in London. It seems unusual that such a lawless character should write a book full of knightly adventures and noble deeds, but the fact that Malory was accused of these crimes does not necessarily mean that he was guilty of them. There is no record of a trial or of sentence being passed upon him.

Some historians, however, believe *Le Morte d'Arthur* was written by Thomas Malory of Studley and Hutton in Yorkshire while he was a prisoner of war in France. It also is possible that its author was yet another Thomas Malory, whose identity remains unknown. All that can be said with certainty is that *Le Morte d'Arthur* is the only medieval romance that has held the imagination of more than five centuries of readers, down to the present day. Skillfully, painstakingly, the prisoner-knight gathered its threads from the countless existing Arthurian romances – English, French, some in verse, others in prose - and this is the story he told.

In the days when Uther Pendragon was king of all England, there lived in Cornwall a mighty duke, the Duke of Tintagel, who had a beautiful wife named Ygrayne. The king fell in love with Ygrayne, and one day when she was a guest in the royal palace, he took her aside and asked her to sleep with him. But Ygrayne refused him. She then told her husband what the king had proposed, and begged him to take her from the palace that night and to ride with her to their castle.

They secretly departed, and when they had gone, the king, in his anger and desire for Ygrayne, fell sick. His knights believed that only one man could cure him of his distress - the wizard Merlin. Merlin was sent for, and when he came to the king, he announced that he could, indeed, make him better and even could arrange an assignation for him with Ygrayne, but there was one condition: "The first night that you shall lie by Ygrayne you shall get a child on her, and when that child is born, then you must deliver it to me for me to nourish and look after."

The king agreed, and then Merlin said to him, "Now make you ready. This night you shall lie with Ygrayne in the castle of Tintagel, and you shall be made by magic to look like the duke, her husband." Thus, in the guise of the duke, the king rode to Tintagel and was welcomed by Ygrayne to her bed. In due time, the baby was born, as Merlin had foretold, and in accordance with the promise King Uther had made, the child was wrapped in cloth of gold and handed over to the care of the wizard. Merlin, in turn, entrusted him to Sir Ector, a trustworthy knight and the lord of fine estates in England and Wales. Sir Ector's wife fed him at her breast, and they called a priest to christen him, and the name they gave him was Arthur.

The years passed, King Uther died, and England stood in danger of civil war because the great barons could not agree on who should succeed him. On Merlin's advice, the Archbishop of Canterbury sent for all the quarreling lords and gentlemen-at-arms to come to London at Christmas and pray to Jesus to show them who had the right to be king. The lords and gentlemen came to London and went to the greatest church there before daybreak to pray and hear Mass. After they had knelt down, there suddenly appeared in the churchyard a large square stone. A blacksmith's anvil was fixed in the marble. And a large sword was implanted in the steel, and the following was written around it in letters of gold: WHOSO PULLETH OUT THIS SWORD OF THIS STONE AND ANVIL IS RIGHTWISE KING BORN OF ALL ENGLAND.

The people marveled, but not one of the lords who struggled with all their might to pull the sword from the anvil could move it.

"The man who can pluck out the sword is not here," the archbishop pronounced. "But do not doubt that God will make him known."

It had been arranged that, on New Year's Day, the lords and knights would ride into the fields outside the city to compete in a tournament, and it happened that two of the knights attending the tournament were the good Sir Ector and his son Kay, who recently had been knighted and was eager to prove his valor. With them was Kay's foster brother, Arthur, acting as his squire. As they rode to the tourney ground, Kay suddenly realized he had left his sword in his father's

London lodgings, and he sent Arthur back to fetch it. But when Arthur arrived, he found the door locked, for the servants had left to see the tournament. Arthur said to himself, "I will ride to the churchyard and take the sword with me that sticks in the stone, for my brother, Sir Kay, shall not be without a sword this day."

As Malory tells it: "So whan he cam to the chircheyard, sir Arthur alight and tayed his hors to the style, and so he wente to the tente and found no knyghtes there, for they were atte justyng. And so he handled the swerd by the handels, and lightly and fiersly pulled it out of the stone, and took his hors and rode his way untyll he came to his broder sir Kay and delyverd hym the swerd."

As soon as he saw the sword, Sir Ector understood what Arthur had done and immediately rode with him back to London, where he told him to place the sword back in the anvil and pull it out again. Arthur did so, and although all the lords thereafter tried to do as he did, none could move the sword but Arthur. After that, the people cried out, "We will have Arthur for our king. We will have no more delay. It is God's will that he shall be our king, and we will kill any man who holds against it."

Then they knelt before him, rich and poor alike. Malory continues: "And Arthur foryaf [forgave] hem and took the swerd bitwene both his handes and offred it upon the aulter where the

Archebisshop was, and so was he made knyghte
of [by] the best man that was there. And so anon
was the coronacyon made, and ther was he sworne
unto his lordes and the comyns [common people]
for to be a true kyng, to stand with true justyce fro
thens forth the dayes of this lyf."

Now that he was king, Arthur set out at the head
of his knights to fight against the evil barons who
were oppressing his people and against the rebel
lords who would not accept his right to the crown.
Among these rebel lords was King Lot of Lothian
and Orkney, who refused to recognize as king a
beardless boy who was not of royal blood. While
Arthur was at war in Wales, Lot's wife, Morgause,
came to his headquarters in the city of Caerleon,
pretending to bring him a message, but her intent
was to spy on him.

Queen Morgause was the daughter of Ygrayne
and the Duke of Tintagel, meaning she was
Arthur's half-sister. But Arthur did not know this,
and when Morgause came to him with her four
young sons - Agravaine, Gaheris, Gareth, and
Gawain - she was so beautiful, richly dressed, and
desirable, Arthur "cast great love unto her and
desired to lie by her." And so they were agreed, and
he begat upon his sister a child, and the name of
the child was Mordred.

Soon after their encounter, King Arthur was riding
with Merlin beside a lake. He had broken his sword

in the fighting, but Merlin told him to ignore his concerns – "hereby is a sword that shall be yours if I can." Then in the middle of the lake, an arm appeared out of the water. In its hand was a shining sword. Catching sight of a young woman walking by the lake, he said to her, "Damsel, what sword is that yonder that the arm holds above the water? I would it were mine, for I have no sword."

"Sir Arthur," replied the damsel, "that sword is mine, and you shall have it. Go into yonder barge and row yourself to the sword and take it and the scabbard with you." Arthur did as she instructed, and he called the sword Excalibur, which means "cut steel."

Armed with Excalibur, Arthur sailed across the Channel to fight the Roman Emperor Lucius, who had demanded a tribute that the English were not prepared to pay. Along the way, he stopped to save the people of Normandy from the giant of Mont-St.-Michel, whom he found gnawing on the roasted limbs of newborn children. "There was never devil in hell more horriblier made" than this giant, who was thirty feet tall and the foulest sight that anyone had ever seen. He snatched up an iron club and swiped at Arthur so hard his crown fell off. But Arthur grappled with him, "and so they weltered and tumbled over the crags and bushes" until they finally rolled down the mount to the seashore. There,

Arthur plunged a dagger into the giant's ribs and killed him.

Then Arthur marched south into the province of Champagne, and in a great battle there, he overwhelmed the Emperor Lucius and killed him with his own hands. With his army, he traveled onward over the mountains into Italy, overcoming all enemies, Saracens, and monsters as he marched and was crowned emperor in Rome by the pope. On his return to England, he was met by his court, who escorted him in triumph to Camelot.

King Arthur's knights had long been pressing him to take a wife. When the king sought Merlin's advice, the magician asked him if there was any woman he loved more than another.

"Yea," said King Arthur, "I love Guinevere, daughter of King Leodegrance of Cameliard who holds in his house the Round Table that was given to him by my father, King Uther; and Guinevere is the fairest damsel that I know or could ever find." But Merlin, who had the gift of seeing into the future, warned Arthur against Guinevere. He insisted that she would not be faithful to her husband but fall in love with his noblest knight, and that this knight, Sir Lancelot, would fall in love with her. Arthur paid no attention; he was determined to marry Guinevere. So Merlin went to King Leodegrance of Cameliard to tell him of Arthur's desire.

"That is the best tidings that ever I heard," said King Leodegrance, who esteemed Arthur as a most noble and worthy king. "I shall send him a gift that shall please him, for I shall give him the Round Table which Uther, his father, gave me. There are places at it for 150 knights, and I shall fill 100 of those places myself by sending him a hundred good knights."

"Now, Merlin," said King Arthur when he heard this news, "go and find me 50 knights of the most courage and renown in all this land." And Merlin went forth, but he brought only twenty-eight knights back to Camelot because he could find no more who were worthy to sit at the Round Table. One of them was Arthur's nephew Gawain, who was to be knighted on the day of the wedding. And Guinevere and King Arthur were married in the church of St. Stephen at Camelot.

The Archbishop of Canterbury then was sent for to bless the seats of the Round Table while all the knights were in their places. After they had risen and gone to pay homage to King Arthur, the seat of each chair was engraved in golden letters with the name of the knight to whom the place belonged, except for two seats, which had no names. Merlin told the king that no knight should sit in those places but those who were worthiest. Each knight was given money and land, and was charged by Arthur never to commit murder, robbery, or any evil deed; grant mercy to those who requested it; and, upon pain of death, help ladies in distress.

All the knights promised to obey these laws, and all of them were brave and noble men. Yet one stood out above all the others due to his nobility and courage - Sir Lancelot of the Lake, son of the King of Benwick. As Merlin had foretold, he performed many chivalrous acts for Queen Guinevere, "whom he loved above all other ladies all the days of his life." And the queen fell in love with him.

But King Arthur did not know of their affection for one another, and he and Lancelot and Lancelot's son, Galahad, and Tristan, Gawain, Gareth, Percival, Bors, and Bedivere and all the other members of the noble fellowship undertook many adventures and quests. They sought to slay the Questing Beast. They laid siege to castles. They took part in dangerous battles and exciting tournaments. They strove to gain the love of ladies, and above all, they endeavored to find the Holy Grail, the vessel used by Christ at the Last Supper. It had mysteriously appeared one evening at Camelot, covered in white silk, and after filling the hall where the king and his knights sat with brilliant light and sweet perfumes, it disappeared. Nearly all the knights joined in the quest for the Holy Grail, to the sorrow both of Arthur, who feared they would never return to the Round Table, and Guinevere, who grieved to see them - in particular,

Lancelot - depart from Camelot. Although Lancelot tried with all his strength of body and mind, although he did penances, humbled himself, and wore a hairshirt for more than a year, he never could do more than glimpse the Holy Grail from a distance, for no knight could complete the quest who was not free from sin. Only Galahad, Percival, and Bors were pure enough to be worthy, and after they successfully found the Grail, the sacred vessel was borne up to heaven and never seen again.

However hard Lancelot had tried to forget his passion for the queen, he found that he could not banish her from his thoughts. Soon after his return from the Grail quest, they were meeting secretly once more. "So they loved together more hotter than they did before and had many such secret trysts together that many in the court of Camelot spoke of it." Loudest in their talk against the queen and Lancelot were Gawain's brother, Agravaine, and his half-brother, Mordred, the king's son. One day in the king's chamber, Agravaine said openly, "I marvel that we all be not ashamed both to see and to know how Lancelot lies daily and nightly by the queen. Fall whatsoever fall may, I will disclose it to the king."

True to his threat, Agravaine, accompanied by Mordred, went to the king and told him what people were whispering about the queen and Lancelot and urged him to set a trap to catch them. "My lord," said Agravaine, "you shall ride to-morrow a-hunting, and doubt you not, Lancelot will not go with you. And so when it draws toward night, send word to the queen that you will stay out all night, and send for your cooks. And then upon pain of death that night, we shall take him with the queen, and we shall bring him to you, alive or dead."

Arthur was loath to believe them, but in the end, he agreed. The next morning, he went hunting and sent word to the queen that he would be out all night. Agravaine and Mordred and twelve other knights who were jealous of Lancelot hid in a chamber next door to the queen's apartments and waited for her lover to join her. Once he was inside the room, his enemies rushed to the door and cried out, "You traitor, Sir Lancelot, now you are taken! Come out of the queen's chamber!"

Lancelot had no weapon but his sword, but he was determined not to be taken. He wrapped his cloak around his sword arm and called through the door, "Now, fair lords, leave your noise and your rushing, and I shall set open this door and then you may do with me what you like." He then unbarred the door and opened it a crack so that only one man at a time might get through. The first who came was Sir Calogrenant of Gore, who struck at Lancelot with all his strength, but Lancelot deflected the blow with his thickly wrapped arm and knocked his opponent to the floor.

"Then Sir Lancelot with great might drew the knight within the chamber door, and with the help of the queen and her ladies, was armed in Calogrenant's armor, and set open the chamber door and mightily strode in among the knights. And anon, at the first stroke he slew Sir Agravaine and anon, after, twelve of his fellows, for there was none of the twelve knights might stand Sir Lancelot one buffet. And also he wounded Sir Mordred, and therewithal Mordred fled with all his might . . . to King Arthur . . . wounded and all bloodied.

"'Ah! Jesu, mercy! How may this be?' said the king. 'Took you him in the queen's chamber?'

"'Yea! So God me help!' said Sir Mordred, 'There we found him.' And so he told the king from the beginning to the ending. . . .

"'Alas,' said the king, 'now I am sure the noble fellowship of the Round Table is broken for ever.'"

Overwhelmed with grief, Arthur gave orders that the queen must be burned for treason in accordance with the laws of England. Gawain pleaded with his uncle not to do so, but Arthur would not listen. Gawain refused to be present, and the king commanded his younger brothers, Gaheris and Gareth, to escort the queen to the stake and witness her punishment. They were as reluctant as Gawain, but they were too young to disobey the king's command. In token of their protest, however, they insisted on attending the queen to her execution unarmed.

Guinevere was led to the stake, outside the city of Carlisle, and a priest heard her confession. But just as the fire was about to be lit, Lancelot and a band of his compatriots galloped up, lashing out with their swords, striking to the ground all those who resisted them. "And in this rushing and hurling, as Sir Lancelot pressed hither and thither, it misfortuned him to slay Sir Gaheris and Sir Gareth," whom he did not recognize in the confusion. Then Lancelot cut Guinevere loose from her bonds and rode away with her to his castle, Joyous Garde, where his allies flocked to join him.

When Arthur heard the news and of the death of Gaheris and Gareth, he fainted. When he returned to consciousness, he began to mourn the loss of "the fairest fellowship of noble knights" that a "Christian king ever held together. Within these two days, I have lost nigh forty knights and also the noble fellowship of Sir Lancelot and his blood. And the death of Sir Gaheris and Sir Gareth will cause the greatest mortal war that ever was, for I am sure that when their brother, Sir Gawain, knows thereof I shall never have rest of him till I have destroyed Sir Lancelot. And therefore, wit you well, my heart was never so sorry as it is now. And much more am I sorrier for my good knights' loss than for the loss of my fair queen, for queens I might have enough, but such a fellowship of good knights shall never be together again."

Arthur summoned his knights and laid siege to Lancelot in Joyous Garde. There were many battles, but in all Lancelot held back and would not fight his hardest, because he loved Arthur and had no heart to crush him. At last, the pope interceded to arrange a truce by which Arthur would forgive Guinevere and take her back. But Gawain would not allow the king to forgive Lancelot. Thus, Lancelot was banished to his kingdom of Benwick in France, and Arthur and Gawain crossed the Channel with 60,000 men to make war on him there.

In Arthur's absence, Mordred, who had been appointed regent of England and guardian of Queen Guinevere, seized his chance to replace his father on the throne. He pretended that he had received a letter announcing Arthur's death and called a parliament and had himself chosen king and crowned at Canterbury. Then he rode to Winchester and told Guinevere he would marry her.

But Guinevere fled to London and took up residence in the Tower of London, "and suddenly in all haste possible she stuffed it with all manner of victual, and well garnished it with men, and so kept it. Then Sir Mordred was passing wroth out of measure. And a short tale for to make, he went and laid a mighty siege about the Tower of London, and made many great assaults, and threw many great engines unto them and shot great guns."

When news came that Arthur was returning home, Mordred had to lift the siege and make for Dover to oppose the landing of his father's troops. At Dover, "there was much slaughter of gentle knights and many a bold baron was laid full low." But both Arthur and Mordred survived to fight again, and on that day, there was "never seen a more dolefuller battle in no Christian land." From morning until night, the fighting raged until 100,000 noble knights lay dead upon the field. "Then was King Arthur wroth out of measure when he saw his people so slain, and he looked about him and was aware where stood Sir Mordred leaning upon his sword among a great heap of dead men."

Gripping his spear in both hands, he ran at Mordred, crying, "Traitor! Now is thy death day come!" He plunged his spear into Mordred's stomach beneath the shield, and its point passed through Mordred's body. Mortally wounded, Mordred raised his sword and struck his father so ferocious a blow upon the helmet that the steel edge cut through the visor and entered Arthur's skull.

"And noble Arthur fell in a swoon to the earth, and there he swooned oftentimes." Bedivere, the last of his knights still alive, although he, too, was grievously wounded, knelt down and held the king in his arms.

"My time passes fast, Sir Bedivere," King Arthur said. "Take my good sword, Excalibur, and go with it to yonder water's side and throw it into the water."

Bedivere went to the lake and hurled Excalibur as far across the water as he could. As it fell, a hand came up to grasp it by the handle and waved it three times in farewell before taking it under the surface. Bedivere then took the king upon his back and carried him to the water's edge, where a barge stood in which sat many fair ladies wearing black veils and weeping bitterly.

"Now put me into that barge," said King Arthur, "For I must go into the . . . [veil] of Avalon to heal me of my grievous wound. And if thou hear nevermore of me, pray for my soul." Sir Bedivere put the king down gently, laying his head upon the lap of one of the ladies, and the barge sailed into the mists, and King Arthur was heard of no more.

"Yet some men say in many parts of England King Arthur is not dead but had by the will of our Lord Jesus into another place. And men say that he shall come again and he shall win the Holy Cross. And many say this was inscribed upon the tomb: HIC IACET ARTHURUS, REX QUONDAM REXQUE FUTURUS. (Here lies King Arthur, the Once and Future King.)

3
THE LIFE OF ARTHUR

The Holy Grail was introduced into the Arthurian legend by Chrétien de Troyes in the twelfth century, but it was French poet Robert de Boron who introduced the Grail as the chalice containing the blood of Christ crucified, which can only be looked upon by those free of sin. The Grail is often associated with the chalice passed during The Last Supper in the *Gospel of Matthew*; however, its only mention in the Bible is this passage: "And He took a cup and when He had given thanks He gave it to them saying 'Drink this, all of you; for this is My blood of the covenant, which is poured out for many for the forgiveness of sins. I tell you, I shall not drink again of the fruit of the vine until I drink it new with you in My Father's kingdom.'"

According to some accounts, a place of honor at Arthur's Round Table was reserved for the knight who claimed the Holy Grail. Lancelot, because of his affair with Guinevere, was excluded. The quest fell to his son.

Galahad, though himself innocent, was born of deception. His mother, Elaine of Corbenic, was the daughter of King Pelles, also known as the Fisher King, the latest in a long line charged with keeping the Holy Grail. Infatuated with the White Knight upon his arrival in Camelot, Elaine plots to draw him to her bed. When she learns of his love for Guinevere, she enlists a servant girl to trick Lancelot into mistaking Elaine for his queen. The knight is plied with wine; meanwhile, Elaine steals a ring belonging to Guinevere and slips it on her own finger. That night, Galahad is conceived. When Guinevere discovers the affair, she shuns Lancelot, causing him to go insane with grief. Elaine finds the knight in her garden and, to cure his madness, has him gaze upon the Holy Grail through a veil. Returning to his senses, he and Elaine live for several years as man and wife. Galahad, reunited with his father as an adult, is knighted by Lancelot. At Camelot, the son takes the empty seat at the Round Table and soon after embarks on his quest.

Chivalry alone could not win the Grail; this was a spiritual quest. Galahad's first test arrives in the form of a red sword, lodged in a slab of marble washed up on the shore of Camelot. The stone is inscribed: "Never shall man take me hence but only he by whose side I ought to hang; and he shall be the best knight of the world." Lancelot refuses even to touch the sword's hilt. Gawain, Arthur's nephew, fails to budge it, and Lancelot warns that the sword will someday hurt him. But Galahad withdraws it easily. Armed only with this sword, Galahad sets out in search for the Grail. Five days into his journey, Galahad claims a shield – white with a red cross, painted with the blood of Joseph of Arimathea – which could only be carried by him.

Galahad's Grail quest spans five years. At the same time, others among King Arthur's knights set out on their own to claim the cup for themselves. Gawain hopes to find and accompany Galahad, but instead is joined by Gaheris and Yvain the Bastard.

Gawain and Galahad pass each other at the Castle of Maidens, where seven brothers held a number of women captive, and had slain many knights who had attempted to rescue them. Galahad fights the brothers, who, while fleeing the castle, encounter Gawain and his companions, and are killed. That night, a hermit rebukes Gawain for his excessive brutality and advises him to abandon his quest and return to Camelot. But Gawain, blinded by his ambition, and mystified so that he is unable to recognize his fellow knights of the Round Table, slays them one by one – eighteen in all, including Yvain. When he finds Galahad, the two no longer know each other. Striking with his red sword, Galahad strikes Gawain's head, fulfilling Lancelot's prophecy about the weapon.

Galahad meets every challenge on his Grail quest with ease. He dispatches every enemy and performs miracles, healing the sick and banishing demons. After five years of searching for the Grail castle, which magically never appears in the same place, he finds it. He enters the castle with two other knights, Perceval and Bors, who had stood up to their own trials and proven themselves worthy. The castle at Corbenic is familiar to both Perceval, who first glimpsed the Grail here during a Mass, and Galahad, whose grandfather Pelles was its king. After fulfilling another prophecy - mending a sword broken into two pieces - Galahad is entrusted with taking the Grail to the spiritual palace of Sarras. In the Grail, Galahad sees a vision of heaven and wishes for death so that he can enter that kingdom. His wish is granted, and he ascends to heaven along with the Grail, never to be seen again.

Since stories of the Holy Grail began circulating in the twelfth century, belief in its existence and curiosity about its whereabouts have never ceased. Several churches have claimed ownership of the Grail, but most historians agree it resides in the Holy

Grail Chapel of the St. Mary of Valencia Cathedral in Spain. This chalice – a hemispherical cup of dark red agate, with a knobbed stem and two curved handles – is about seven inches tall, less than four inches in diameter, and is inscribed along its base in Arabic. In 1960, Spanish archaeologist Antonio Beltrán inspected the chalice, and determined that it was made between the fourth century B.C. and first century A.D. The Roman Catholic Church has embraced it as the Holy Grail; it has been the official chalice for many popes, as late as Pope Benedict XVI in 2006.

Others believe the Grail is guarded by an ancient order of protectors. Because of their prominence in the eleventh and twelfth centuries when the Grail stories emerged, many believe the Knights Templar are the guardians of the Grail. Among the most skilled fighting men of the Crusades, the Knights Templar were distinguished by their shields – white and emblazoned with a red cross, like that carried by Galahad in the Arthurian legend. The Knights' disbandment in 1312 only fueled speculation and legends about their secret and most holy responsibility. Another legend holds that the Grail was returned to Camelot, and is buried deep in the spring at Glastonbury Hill, which in Arthur's time was the monastery of Avalon.

These players and theories add richness, romance, and magic to the legend of Arthur told by Sir Thomas

Malory. Based on earlier French romances, which were based on Geoffrey of Monmouth's *History of the Kings of Britain*, which, in turn, was based on earlier records, legends, and oral traditions, the story is far removed from the harsh reality of the fifth century and from the threatened island of Britain in which the real Arthur was born

4
CENTURY OF CONFLICT

U nderstanding Arthur requires an understanding of the politics and plights of fifth-century Britain.

The Roman Empire was disintegrating. For years, Rome had been defending its frontiers, which stretched some 10,000 miles, from the North Sea along the Rhine to the Danube to the shores of the Black Sea; and from Constantinople to the Strait of Gibraltar, then northward through Spain and Gaul to Britain. But the once-civilized and disciplined Roman way of life had become decadent. Rome's emperors were merely puppets in the hands of their generals, who frequently assassinated them and took their places on the throne. The administration that had enabled the Roman government to keep control of an unwieldy conglomeration of nations and provinces had degenerated into a bureaucracy riddled with corruption. Trade declined as taxes increased. The Roman army, once noted for its legions of well-equipped soldiers, now consisted of troops of mercenaries, hired to defend the empire against steadily increasing pressure from other forces - Goths, Huns, Saxons, Vandals - moving southward and westward from Scandinavia, the lands around the Baltic, and the Russian steppes.

In 429, under the leadership of their cunning and ruthless King Gaiseric, a horde of Vandals poured out of Spain into Roman Africa, the main source of Rome's corn supply and home of a prosperous civilization. They made their way along the North African coast, conquering and pillaging as they went, and in 439, captured Carthage, Rome's great African seaport. Gaiseric built a huge pirate fleet, and using Carthage as their base; the Vandals began to ravage the Roman cities around the Mediterranean Sea and to threaten Rome itself.

Already endangered by hostile forces along its northern and eastern frontiers, Rome no longer could offer any protection to distant Britain. One legion after another was called back to fight Rome's wars on the Continent until only a small garrison remained. By 410, most had withdrawn, and by the middle of the century, Roman power had effectively ended. The islanders were left to fend for themselves.

For almost a century, Britain had been under intermittent attack. From the north, fierce, tattooed Picts came down from the Caledonian mountains of Scotland. In the second century A.D., the Emperor Hadrian had built a wall from east to west between the River Tyne and the Solway Firth to keep the Picts out of the Romanized country farther south. But once the legions that had defended it were gone, the Picts clambered over the abandoned ramparts and swarmed south toward the Humber. The Picts were followed by the Scotti, marauders from Ireland, who sailed across the Irish Sea in their light skin-and-wood boats called currachs. They pillaged the western coasts of England and Wales, terrifying the fishermen and farmers, spearing and stabbing those who could not escape, and setting fire to their thatched-roof huts. The Saxons were more aggressive than either the Picts or the Irish war bands.

The people commanded expanding nations that were no longer content with their restricted farmlands on the Continental mainland. As Roman power declined in Britain, they began to look west for a richer land on which to settle. They crossed the North Sea in long, shallow-draught galleys constructed of overlapping oak planks, curved up at either end, and rowed by a score of warriors. They preferred long hair and beards, wore thick shirts and trousers, and cloaks to which skins were sewn to give them extra warmth when they were used as blankets at night. As well as their seax, or short-swords, they carried thick, iron-spiked spears, battle-axes, and round wooden shields covered with hide. Few of them wore helmets. They were ruthless, violent men, and all along the southern and eastern coasts of Britain, they pillaged and looted, raped and murdered, burning farms, killing livestock, then sailing home.

Late-fourth-century Britain was still one of the most pleasant provinces of the Western Roman Empire, though no longer as prosperous as it had been. The rolling plains of the south and west were dotted with the stucco-and-brick villas of gentlemen-farmers - although many had been abandoned, their brightly painted walls crumbling into ruins. In winter, the well-furnished rooms of these villas had been warmed by heated flues that ran beneath their mosaic floors; in summer, fountains played in the courtyards and grapevines grew against garden walls. Outside their gates, roads still led to the towns that had been Rome's chief contribution to the British way of life - towns whose paved streets and imposing buildings were constructed in the regular, rectilinear manner favored by the architects of the eternal city.

Roads intersected the island, linking northern fortress with southern port, garrison with tribal capital, stretching from the forts along Hadrian's Wall to the clustered villas of the South Downs, from the legionary fortress at Chester in the west to the large town of Caistor-next-Norwich on the east coast. And at the center of this complex of roads stood Londinium, one of the most impressive cities north of the Alps.

Roman London was a city of some 30,000 inhabitants, living in an area of more than 300 acres enclosed by three miles of strong stone walls, nine feet thick, up to twenty feet high, and pierced by gates where the main roads led through them. The river gate, which faced the traveler as he came across the wide, wooden bridge spanning the Thames, opened onto the street leading up to the Basilica, the center of commerce and government, a vast and impressive building more than 420 feet long, with high arcaded walls. Just inside this river gate were the public baths, and down the streets on either side were the wide, arched fronts of numerous shops and counting houses, and the porticoed homes of prosperous merchants.

Life in Londinium, like life in the other big towns of Roman Britain, was well-organized and pleasant for all but the poor and the slaves. The farms outside the walls, and the gardens within them, produced meat, vegetables, and fruit; potable water, piped in hollowed tree trunks, was plentiful; the Thames, whose wharves moored scores of trading ships, was full of salmon and trout and shoals of fresh-water fish. There was no shortage of work. Brickfields, potteries, and glassworks, joiners' shops and mills, masons' yards and furniture factories, as well as row upon row of warehouses and work sheds lined the riverfront. Latin was the universal language, written as well as spoken. The citizens of Londinium prided themselves in being more civilized than the Germanic pirates and raiders from across the sea - barbarians who worshiped gods of war, who feared and believed unfamiliar towns were places where evil spirits dwelt.

The Britons, Romanized and peaceable, were no match for these invaders. Although they still were held together by strong tribal loyalties and customs, they no longer possessed the warlike spirit that had inspired the Iceni tribe when they followed their Queen Boudica into battle against Roman conquerors in the reign of the Emperor Nero. Accustomed for centuries to relying on the empire's legions to protect them, the Britons now were incapable of defending themselves, and as the fourth century drew to its close, they grew ever more in need of protection.

The Saxons, an increasing menace, had established bases along the Continental coast from which they could raid Britain more easily. In the west, the Scotti were an increasing threat under High King Niall of the Nine Hostages; in repeated raids hundreds of prisoners were carried off to become the slaves of Irish chieftains. Niall's forces invaded as far inland as Chester, Caerleon-on-Usk, and Wroxeter. In 405, Niall was killed at sea, but the raids continued.

After the legions had gone, and the Vandals had begun to swarm across Roman Africa under King Gaiseric, Roman Britain had not lost all hope of survival. In 429, a bishop named Germanus arrived from Auxerre in Gaul. He had been a soldier in his youth and never had lost his taste for battle. Germanus found Britain a "most wealthy island," with thriving communities governed by local kings whose families had been used to kingship from ancient times. Even before the Romans occupied Britain permanently in 43 A.D., Cunobelinus, the powerful ruler of the Catuvellauni tribe in southern Britain, used to style himself *rex*, or king, on the coins issued from his mint. With the breakdown of Roman rule, the Britons tended to honor ancient ties and rally around their regional leaders.

Despite the constant inroads by the barbarians, Germanus found that town life continued. Trade in the port of Londinium remained active; in Verulamium, farther north, the Roman theater had become a refuse dump for decaying market vegetables, but shops were open and local businesses flourished. Germanus also found that while the invaders might destroy isolated farms near the coast, burn the huts of peasants and fishermen, trample orchards and vineyards, they were not capable of fighting a pitched battle or storming the stone walls of a Roman town or fort.

Before his arrival in Britain, Germanus had been military governor of the Armorican district of Gaul, charged with guarding the Channel coast. It was not as a soldier, though, that he had been sent to Britain, but as a preacher who could combat a new heresy called Pelagianism. A Briton named Pelagius had begun to teach that the soul is born in a neutral state and that the human will was free to make its choice between virtue and vice. This idea denied the concept of original sin, and the bishops of Rome feared such teaching might undermine the authority of the church. Germanus, however, was as concerned with the bodies of the British people as with their souls.

He reorganized the bands of local militia, persuaded their leaders to appoint him their supreme commander, and taught them how to fight a formal battle. When the barbarians appeared, the Britons, instead of retreating inland, withdrew in a disciplined fashion and drew their enemies into the trap that Germanus had laid for them. The unsuspecting Saxons marched into a narrow valley, and when they had gone too far to retreat, Germanus cried, "Alleluia!" The Britons took up the cry and rushed down both sides of the valley onto their foes. The Saxons fled, dropping their spears as they ran.

It was a great victory, but only a temporary respite. As the years passed, the Saxons and their allies grew more resolute and enterprising. They came now not only in galleys but also in ships with leather sails, concealing their vessels in coastal inlets and using neglected roads to advance into the British countryside. They became expert at besieging and storming fortified encampments. They soon began to settle in the land they had previously been intent on pillaging and established small farming settlements around the wooden halls of their thanes, or lords.

In 446, the Britons made a final plea for help from Rome. Those parts of Romanized Britain that still were able to act collectively dispatched an urgent message to Aetius, the Roman general in Gaul: "To Aetius, three times consul, the groans of the Britons; the barbarians drive us to the sea, the sea drives us to the barbarians; between these two forms of death, we are either massacred or drowned."

But there was no response. Aetius was occupied fighting barbarians in Gaul. No help came.

Then - or so it seems from the confused and incomplete records of these times - a call was made to Vortigern, a powerful ruler who had gained control of an extensive district in the west of Britain and who exercised considerable influence over the south of the island as well. According to some historians, Vortigern married Sevira, daughter of the Roman Emperor Magnus Maximus, and though a rough, British-speaking overlord himself, he had some respect for Roman ways. His advice to the Britons was to employ a Roman solution.

To maintain its power, the Roman Empire had relied not only upon recruits taken into its army from all the world's races, but also upon entire tribes enlisted to defend particular areas. These tribes, or foederati, were admitted into the empire in return for defending whatever portion of it they were allotted; although the soldiers gained land within the empire, they maintained their own laws and customs and their own identities. This policy, Vortigern apparently suggested - and the British councilors agreed - should be adopted now. In return for their help in keeping the Pitts and Scotti and any other raiders at bay, and on the understanding that they live at peace with their British neighbors, a war band of Saxon troops and their women were accepted, and they settled in the southeastern region of Britain.

Venerable Bede, the Northumbrian monk and historian whose *Ecclesiastical History of the English Church and People*, completed in 731, is our chief source of information for this period, tells us that the leaders of the federated troops, Jute chiefs named Hengist and Horsa, established themselves on the Isle of Thanet, an area of fertile farmland separated from Kent by a narrow channel, which was guarded at each end by a Roman fort. The area was a long way from the parts of Britain under attack by the Picts and the Irish war bands, but it was convenient for Vortigern to keep them under his control when they were not fighting in the north, and the Saxons were well placed to undertake coastal patrols for the protection of Londinium.

At first, Britain was successful. The Picts and Scotti were subdued, the Kentish settlement prospered, and Britain enjoyed a period of unaccustomed peace. But the settlers gradually called friends and reinforcements - Angles, Jutes, and Saxons - from across the North Sea and began spreading themselves deeper into southeastern Britain, demanding more land and greater payments. At some time in the 450s, the angry quarrels between them and their British employers flared into open war. At a ferocious battle at Crayford in Kent in 457, the Britons lost 4,000 men on the field and "fled to London in great terror."

This event is the last recorded mention of London for a century and a half. Britain's capital and other Roman towns fell victim to the invaders, now armed with Roman siege equipment. The Saxons advanced inland, devastating countryside and towns alike: "Public and private buildings were razed [according to Bede], priests were slain at the altar; bishops and people alike, regardless of rank, were destroyed with fire and sword, and none remained to bury those who had suffered a cruel death. A few wretched survivors captured in the hills were butchered wholesale, and others, desperate with hunger, came out and surrendered to the enemy for food, although they were doomed to lifelong slavery even if they escaped instant massacre. Some fled overseas in their misery; others, clinging to their homeland, eked out a wretched and fearful existence."

Bede's picture is a fearful one, yet the vast majority of survivors, in discomfort and misery, probably stayed close to what once had been their homes. Some may have sailed across the Channel to the old Roman province of Armorica, the first stage of three centuries of migration that eventually took a British (Celtic) language - and gave the modern name of Brittany - to this great Atlantic peninsula.

In the west, tribal leader Ambrosius Aurelianus stood against the Saxon threat and offered shelter to those who had escaped or were prepared to take up arms in defense of the old culture. He advised Vortigern of the dangers of the Saxon alliance and managed to avoid its consequences.

Ambrosius was of Roman descent, and the land he ruled was certainly as Romanized as any in Britain. Although the Saxon warrior Aelle landed near Selsey in 477 and carved out the kingdom of the South Saxons (the present-day county of Sussex), and in 495, Cerdic landed on the shore of Southampton Water to found the kingdom of the West Saxons (later King Alfred the Great's kingdom of Wessex), the Romano-British kingdom of Ambrosius remained secure. To this haven, says a sixth-century British historian and monk named Gildas, men from the other threatened tribes of Britain flocked "as eagerly as bees when a storm is brewing."

For some time, Ambrosius prevented conflict in his kingdom. A contemporary writer on the Continent described Britain in the 480s as prosperous and peaceful despite the Saxon incursions. By 500, there was a considerable settlement of Saxons along the east coast, and the kingdoms of Sussex and Wessex continued to flourish and expand. Yet in the Cotswold Hills, along the borders of Wales, and in Dumnonia (occupied today by the counties of Devon and Cornwall) Roman Britain lived on.

Although written records and archaeological evidence from this time in Britain are sparse, it is possible to build a credible picture of what life was like in the western area of Britain loyal to Ambrosius.

Some sort of seaborne trade was maintained with such Atlantic ports as Bordeaux and Nantes, and with the Mediterranean - increasingly so after about 500. Small amounts of wine in amphorae, and perhaps cooking oil as well, came in the ships of the traders. Early writings suggest that corn, woolen goods, hides, Irish wolfhounds (which were prized for their speed and strength), and slaves were exported in return.

In centers like Gloucester, life may have continued according to Roman customs. But in most of Ambrosius' kingdom, people had reverted to a less Romanized way of life, grouped in small communities similar to the hill forts of their ancestors and speaking a variety of British dialects. For the poor life was difficult. Living in stone-and-thatch huts, tilling small fields to improve their diet of bread and occasional pieces of meat with herbs, such people still valued their freedom and sense of national identity - and were prepared to fight for them.

Perhaps to protect themselves against Saxon invasion and their cattle from raids, either by the Saxons or other British tribes, the inhabitants of this last enclave of Romano-British civilization built a series of linear earthworks. One of the largest of these is the Wansdyke, a man-made ridge that stretches fifty miles from Inkpen in what is now Berkshire, across Savernake Forest and the Marlborough Downs, over a Roman road that used to lead into Bath, on toward the Bristol Channel. Historians are uncertain of its purpose, but its presence, rising up from the peaceful fields of the modern English countryside, is a reminder of some tremendous effort by people who had only the most primitive implements to aid them.

Under Ambrosius, the Britons may have occasionally lost ground, but they never were driven into retreat. They had a cause and a leader. But once he died, succession was a concern. Could anyone replace Ambrosius? Could any man be a more effective leader?

With their warrior king dead, the Britons' need for a leader in their struggle against the Saxons was answered by a young man whose ability would make him into a legend - Arthur.

5
ARTHUR AT WAR

"In those days [that followed the death of Ambrosias] the Saxons grew in numbers and prospered in Britain. . . . Then Arthur the warrior and the kings of the Britons fought against the Saxons, but Arthur himself was the dux bellorum, the commander in the battles. The first battle was on the mouth of the river which is called Glein. The second, the third, the fourth, and the fifth upon another river, which is called Dubglass, and is in the region of Linnuis. The sixth battle was upon the river which is called Bassas.

"The seventh battle was in the wood of Celidon - that is, Cat Coit Celidon. The eighth was the battle by the castle of Guinnion, in which Arthur carried upon his shoulders an image of the

Blessed Mary, the Eternal Virgin. And the heathen were turned to flight on that day, and great was the slaughter brought upon them through the virtue of our Lord, Jesus Christ, and through the virtue of the Blessed Virgin, His Mother.

"The ninth battle was fought in the City of the Legion. The tenth battle was waged on the banks of the river which is called Tribruit. The eleventh battle was fought in the mountain which is called Agned. The twelfth battle was on Mount Badon where in one day nine hundred and sixty men fell in one onslaught of Arthur's. And no one laid them low but himself alone. And in all these battles he stood out as victor."

Thus, Arthur makes his first appearance in the historical record. Its compiler was the Welsh monk Nennius, writing in the ninth century; the work is the same *Historia Brittonum* that relates the "marvels" of the stone that bears the footprint of Arthur's dog Cavall and of the mysterious mound that marks the grave of Arthur's son Anir.

Although these marvels may defy belief, Nennius is more credible when he lists these twelve victories won by Arthur as commander of British forces. While some of the places named are no longer identifiable, some others might be pinpointed, based on ninth-century Welsh names. It is impossible to identify the sites of Castle Guinnion, the mountain called Agned, or the River Bassas, but it has been assumed that the region of Linnuis could be the Lindsey area of Lincolnshire south of the Humber, and that the River Glein is the Lincolnshire River Glen. This would support the belief that Arthur may have campaigned against the Saxons and Angles who were landing on the east coast of Britain in the early sixth century - giving their name to the area now known as East Anglia. The wood of Celidon is probably the forest of Caledonia in the wild Scottish uplands beyond Hadrian's Wall, where a campaign against the Picts was fought about this time. The City of the Legion is probably Chester. Mount Badon has been variously identified with Badbury near Swindon in Wiltshire, Badbury Hill in Berkshire, Badbury Rings near Blandford in Dorset, and Bedwyn near Inkpen - but in any case, it is believed to be in southern Britain near the Wansdyke. Wherever it was, Mount Badon was clearly the site of an important battle or siege. Arthur's troops likely surrounded the steep and fortified hill, cutting off the enemy's supplies, forcing them to break out, then attacking them as they tried to escape.

Because the list of battles appears to range so widely across the country, some historians believe all the battles took place in one area - the north, for instance, or the southwest. But if they ranged across Britain, this would bear out Nennius' description of Arthur as a *dux bellorum*: a supreme military leader who took his army from coast to coast fighting invaders whenever and wherever they seemed most threatening.

Arthur's defense of Britain may have been based on a system developed by the Romans in the previous century, when the island was divided into four provinces and its military organization into three commands. The *Dux Britanniarum* (the Duke of the Britains), who had his headquarters at York, was responsible for defending the northern frontier against the Picts and Scotti; the *Comes Litoris Saxonici* (the Count of the Saxon Shore) defended the southeastern coast from Germanic pirates aided by forts that stretched from the Wash to the Isle of Wight. Both these leaders commanded a local militia who were charged with defending the frontier line. The third leader, the *Comes Britanniarum* (the Count of the Britains) was entrusted with a field army of six cavalry and three infantry units, a mobile army that was able to come to the defense of his colleagues when the need arose.

The army under the count's command was chiefly cavalry. The early Roman army had made little use of cavalry, preferring to rely on its infantry, grouped in legions 6,000 strong. Gradually, however, as the Roman generals came in contact with barbarian troops using cavalry armed with bows and spears, they incorporated cavalry into their commands. These were, usually, lightly armed foederati, but there were also mailed cavalry, known as cataphracti or Clibanarii. The cataphracts, whose name comes from a Greek word meaning "covered in mail," wore helmets and body armor made of iron scales or chain mail, with arm and leg pieces attached. The Clibanarii, so called from the Latin word for baking pan, were armed from head to foot in scales or mail, and their horses, too, wore protective iron scales sewn on blankets - a heavy and cumbersome uniform, especially in hot weather. Both types of cavalry were armed with long spears and swords and could slash their way through enemy troops with terrible effect.

As Rome's frontiers demanded a more flexible army, Roman legions were reorganized into smaller units of 1,000 men per legion while the cavalry became a separate arm of the service. Mobility was essential, so the troops could fight where they were needed most.

The situation in Britain also demanded mobility, and it has been suggested that Arthur served in some capacity resembling a count, deploying a small force of cavalry, which may or may not have been armored, but was disciplined and effective in dealing with Saxon foes who had no horses and little organization.

As commander in chief of his band of knights, Arthur would have been directing a campaign that determined Britain's freedom and future. He was the only leader capable of organizing the island's defense against its invaders; the one leader able to inspire his people to fight to the death. But if this were the reason Nennius called him *dux bellorum*, it calls the incidental details in the historian's account into question. Neither his going into battle with an image of the Virgin Mary on his shoulder nor his singlehandedly killing 960 men is easy to accept as fact. But it could be that Nennius misread an old text. The Welsh word for "shoulder," *ysgwydd*, is almost identical with the word for "shield," *ysgwyd*. It seems more probable that Arthur went into battle carrying a shield bearing a badge proclaiming his faith in the Blessed Mother.

As for the number of victims slain by Arthur at Mount Badon, the distinction might be simply that Arthur and his men were fighting this battle alone against the Saxons and that Nennius was describing an overwhelming defeat inflicted by Arthur's cavalry.

The next references to a historical Arthur occur in the *Annales Cambriae*, a Latin list of events and the years in which they took place. These probably were compiled in the north of Britain about the middle of the tenth century, but they come from sources at least as early as those used by Nennius. These "Annals of Wales," which cover the years 453 to 954, mention only the last of Arthur's battles under the date 516: "The battle of Badon in which Arthur carried the cross of Our Lord Jesus Christ, for three days and three nights on his shoulders, and the Britons were victorious." (Again, the reference to Arthur carrying the cross on his shoulders may reflect a Welsh confusion between shoulders and shields.) Under the date 537, there is a second reference to Arthur, this time to the battle fought between him and his illegitimate son Mordred that forms the climax of *Le Morte d'Arthur*: "The battle of Camlann in which Arthur and Medraut were slain; and there was death in England."

At this point, there is no evidence in the record that Arthur was a king. But his name, which in its Latin form is Artorius, suggests that he may have come from a distinguished family in some way connected with Rome. More than one Roman named Artorius lived in Britain during the empire's occupation, and one, Lucius Artorius Castus, led the sixth legion on an expedition to Armorica in the middle of the second century. Some scholars have proposed that an ancestor of the British Arthur may have served under him and that, proud of this service, he gave his son his leader's name, which was handed down from generation to generation. But such a conjecture is not necessary. The name Artorius implies that Arthur was of Roman descent, and the fact that he succeeded Ambrosius as leader implies that Arthur may well have been related to Ambrosius. According to Geoffrey of Monmouth, Ambrosius was Uther Pendragon's brother and therefore Arthur's uncle - although Uther is probably a product of Geoffrey's imagination. Another possibility: that after his triumph over the Saxons, Arthur's men might have named their leader king, following the example of the Roman legions in fourth-century Britain who proclaimed their general, Maximus, emperor.

It is not until the late eleventh century that records show Arthur regularly and unequivocally as a king. Several biographies of Celtic priests and monks, upon whom the Welsh and Britons rely, describe him as a monarch, although they also somewhat freely bestowed the title of saint. In more than one of the biographies, however, Arthur is called a tyrant king and presented as a ruler with little respect for the church, or as a *rex rebellus*, who remains committed to evil until converted by some miracle worked by a saint whose holy career is presented for the reader's admiration. Although few of these tales about Arthur are credible, they show that the monks who wrote them realized any connection with him, however fanciful, would lend credibility to their forgotten, saintly heroes. Their unflattering portrayal of Arthur also may provide a clue to a mysterious omission in the earliest surviving chronicle of the period, implying that the king had in some way offended the church in his fight for Britain's freedom.

This chronicle, *De Excidio et Conquestu Britanniae*, is the work of the sixth-century monk Gildas. He was likely writing a few years after Arthur's death and may have known Arthur – yet he never mentions his name.

Gildas was the son of a minor British chieftain whose small domain in Scotland was overrun by Picts. He and several of his several brothers abandoned their homeland and fled to Wales, where they were given the protection of King Cadwallon ap Cadfan of Gwynedd. Gildas married in Wales, but his wife soon passed away, and he turned to a religious life. At times, he seems to have resided in Ireland, on a remote island in the Bristol Channel, where he lived as a hermit and subsisted on fish and gulls' eggs; in Brittany; and at Glastonbury in Somerset. On his death, he was deemed worthy of canonization.

He wrote his most significant work, the *De Excidio et Conquestu Britanniae*, circa 540 and refers to it as a book of complaints. In it, he castigates his contemporaries for their lack of foresight and their blindness to the lessons of the past and attacks the local kings of Britain for immorality and tyranny. "They have many wives and all of them adulteresses and prostitutes. They often take oaths and always break them. They wage wars, and the wars are unjust on their own countrymen. They hunt down thieves in the countryside, but they have thieves at their own tables, whom they love and load with gifts."

Gildas briefly summarizes the historical events that led up to this state of affairs, and ends his chronicle with the story of a great victory over the Saxons in a battle that was fought in or about 500. This victory, siege of Mount Badon, put an end to foreign wars, though not to civil wars. This decisive battle is the last of the twelve victories attributed to Arthur by Nennius and the bloody conflict in which, according to the Annales Cambriae, Arthur carried the cross of Christ for three days and nights. But Gildas says nothing of Arthur, referring merely to "gallows-birds," the Saxons, who "dipped [their] red and savage tongue in the western ocean." Gildas credits Ambrosius Aurelianus with organizing the British resistance at Badon, after which an unexpected recovery of the island led kings, nobles, priests and commoners to "live orderly according to their several vocations."

This omission led some later historians to believe Arthur never existed. Some suggested that the Arthurian epic was a fabrication, a result of wishful thinking at a time when a national hero was desperately needed. They argued that Gildas did not mention many names in his text, but he did take note of Ambrosius. Why not Arthur, then, if Arthur had won a victory so complete that Britain had been granted peace for almost half a century?

The question has at least two answers, both of which are credible. One is that Gildas may have had good reason for not naming Arthur directly and that he instead mentioned him in an oblique way that his contemporaries would have understood.

In his attacks on the corrupt rulers of his time, Gildas refers to one Welsh king, Cuneglas, as a "despiser of God, an adulterer, and an oppressor of monks." Yet as a youth, Cuneglas had driven "the chariot which carried The Bear." Who was this great man, known as The Bear, who should have a prince drive his chariot? Gildas does not say. But the Celtic word for "bear" is arth or artos.

It is also possible that Gildas did not mention Arthur by name because Arthur, like so many of his contemporaries, had fallen short of the monk's strict ideals in religion and morals.

Like Cuneglas, Arthur might have earned a reputation as an "oppressor of monks." Fighting the Saxons was a costly enterprise, and a war leader presumably must have had to call upon monasteries for money and food for his men and horses. He likely seized what was not given freely. Such impositions could account for the unsympathetic figure Arthur cuts in the stories of later saints' lives.

But the quarrel – if there, indeed, was a quarrel - between Gildas and Arthur may have been personal. According to a biography of Gildas, written in the twelfth century in Llancarfan Abbey, where Gildas once lived, Arthur had killed Hueil, Gildas' eldest brother. Hueil had not gone to Wales, like the rest of his family, but remained in Scotland to inherit his father's lands. He had come, it seems, to some traitorous understanding with the Picts to secure possession of his kingdom. Consequently, Arthur made war on Hueil and killed him, causing Gildas, who had "diligently loved Arthur," to turn against him. A similar account appears in another eleventh-century Welsh tale, which lends credence to the story. If Gildas and Arthur did find themselves on opposite sides in the civil wars that followed the battle of Mount Badon, and that led to the fight between Arthur and Mordred at Camlann, Gildas' reluctance to mention his brother's killer is understandable. He could scarcely deny the triumph of Mount Badon, but he could not bring himself to record the name of the victor. There is also a long-standing tradition that Gildas did, in fact, write about Arthur, but threw the draft of the book that included his name into the sea.

It may not be necessary to find reasons why Arthur's name does not appear in the *De Excidio*. If the battle of Mount Badon was the resounding victory all accounts suggest it was, its details would be well known to the book's readers. Gildas had no need to repeat that Arthur won it - it would have been a fact of life.

By the time Nennius was writing 250 years later, Arthur had been accepted as the victor at Mount Badon and as the paragon of British heroes - not only in Britain proper, but also in Brittany, where so many Britons had fled after the Saxon invasions. The stories of the mighty warrior were embellished and adapted to the taste of the people in whose land they settled. But the basic storyline remained surprisingly close to the Celtic legends and poems of Wales and the British West Country, where Arthur's deeds were treasured and his praises sung. The common people, the descendants of the people Arthur had fought to defend, never lost faith in their champion. Indeed, their belief became more fervent: "If you do not believe me," wrote a twelfth-century French theologian, "go to the realm of Armorica [to Brittany] which is lesser Britain, and preach about the market places and villages that Arthur the Briton is dead as other men are dead, and facts themselves will show you how true is Merlin's prophecy, which says that the ending of Arthur shall be doubtful. Hardly will you escape unscathed, without being overwhelmed by the curses or crushed by the stones of your hearers."

By the twelfth century, Arthur's fame had spread far beyond Britain and Brittany to France, Germany, and Italy. The sixth-century British warrior whose identity had been obscured by the passage of time became one of the most celebrated heroes of the Christian world. To the peasant, he was the just protector who one day would rise again to right their wrongs; to his lord, Arthur was the model of knightly virtue; to all men and women, Arthur's courage offered hope and his prowess, inspiration. Naturally, proof of his existence was sought - yet proof was lacking. Then, in 1191, the skeptics suddenly were confounded by a remarkable discovery.

The find was made at Glastonbury in Somerset - Arthur's traditional realm - known in local lore as the Isle of Avalon, to which Arthur was borne, after the fateful battle of Camlann.

In earlier times, Glastonbury was an island; the waters of the Bristol Channel had reached deep into Somerset, covering the coastline with tidal water amid which hills and ridges stood like islands. At Glastonbury, the Iron Age British of the second century B.C. built villages of timber huts on patches of dry land. The so-called lake village rested on timber platforms, supported by pilings driven into the marsh and peat.

The people who lived there were skillful farmers who grew wheat, barley, peas, and beans. They were also expert carpenters, wood carvers, basket makers, metalworkers, potters, and glassworkers. Although they were under increasing pressure from the Belgae, warrior tribes who had crossed from northeastern Gaul to settle in Britain, they managed to maintain an astonishingly high standard of civilization for more than a century. Then, shortly before the first Romans landed in Britain, in 55 B.C., the village was attacked by Belgae raiders, who destroyed its buildings and killed most of its inhabitants.

The peace Roman power brought to Britain enabled the survivors to move to drier and healthier ground, and Glastonbury probably became the deserted swamp it had been before the lake village was built. Over the centuries, drops in sea level partially drained the marsh. At some point before the end of the sixth century, a monastery was built there. Its monks used to claim that the Glastonbury monastery was the oldest in Britain, and the original abbey church, the Vetusta Ecclesia, a primitive construction of wattle and daub, was shown to the pilgrims who flocked to Glastonbury to see "the source and fountain of all religion" in Britain.

It was shown to William of Malmesbury, widely regarded as the most reliable twelfth-century historian, when he visited Glastonbury sometime between 1125 and 1135. He seems to have had doubts about its age and authenticity, but he was sufficiently impressed by the abbey's ancient documents to maintain that the Church of St. Mary at Glastonbury was "the first church in the kingdom of Britain."

Delighted to have confirmation of their ancient foundation from such a respected authority, the monks at Glastonbury made and circulated several copies of his *De Antiquitate Glastomensis Ecclesiae*. They went on to issue revised editions of the work, still listing William as the author but adding new material embellishing the abbey's history and reputation. One of these revisionist accounts discussed how the abbey had been founded by "no other hands than those of the Disciples of Christ," who had come to England in 63 A.D. to preach the Gospel. The group was led by Joseph of Arimathea, the follower of Jesus who had Christ's body laid to rest in the sepulcher. A British king, impressed by their conduct, gave them land on which to settle at Glastonbury. There they were visited by the Archangel Gabriel, who told them to build a church, the original Vetusta Ecclesia, and dedicate it to the Virgin Mary.

Gradually, as new editions of William's book were issued by succeeding generations of monks, each hand written with considerable care and artistry, further details were added. St. Joseph of Arimathea had brought with him to Glastonbury, if not the Holy Grail itself, at least a pair of vessels, one containing the blood, the other the sweat of Christ, and these vessels had been buried with him in the abbey grounds. At the foot of Glastonbury Tor, the hill that rises above the abbey, Joseph had knelt to pray, leaning on his staff, and the walking stick had taken root and budded. This plant was the origin of the celebrated Glastonbury Thorn, which flowered every year at Christmas.

Although William of Malmesbury never linked the name of Arthur with Glastonbury, it appeared from later versions of his book that the king, a benefactor and patron of the abbey, was buried there, in the grounds that once had been known as the Isle of Avalon.

In his seminal history of England, *De Gestis Regum Anglorum*, William had called Arthur a man "truly worthy to be celebrated . . . since for a long time he sustained the declining fortunes of his country and incited the unbroken spirit of the people to war. Finally, at the battle of Mount Badon, relying upon the image of the Mother of the Lord which he had fixed upon his armour, he made heed single-handed against 900 of the enemy and routed them with incredible slaughter." But William had taken pains to separate the real Arthur from the Celtic legend - those "foolish dreams of deceitful fables," as he called them - and he went on to state that "the grave of Arthur is nowhere known."

The Glastonbury monks, however, cast such concerns aside. Geoffrey of Monmouth's *History of the Kings of Britain* had been completed in 1139, within a few years of William's visit to Glastonbury, and had made the name of Arthur revered throughout the Christian world. Who could blame them for giving authority to the local tradition that Arthur had been laid to rest at Glastonbury? And what Englishman could not feel gratified when, in 1191, it appeared that their faith had been rewarded with evidence?

The story of the monks' discovery began on May 25, 1184, when a fire broke out in the abbey, destroying virtually all its buildings and relics, including the church. Encouraged by King Henry II, who agreed to contribute a substantial sum for the rebuilding of the abbey, the monks began to raise money themselves. They went into the country to beg. They solicited subscriptions from wealthy nobles. They restored many of the relics that had been burned and exhibited them in shrines where pilgrims could bring their offerings. They found the remains of several saints, including bones belonging to St. Patrick, and a skeleton they claimed to be St. Dunstan, a former abbot of Glastonbury and Archbishop of Canterbury - a claim that aroused much indignation at Canterbury, where the monks had been showing St. Dunstan's tomb to pilgrims for more than 200 years.

The Glastonbury monks collected enough money to begin rebuilding on a lavish scale, and by 1186, the first stage of the work was completed with the dedication of a new Lady Chapel. But in 1189, Henry II died, and his successor, Richard I, had no funds or inclination to rebuild abbeys in England while there were Saracens to fight in the Holy Land. But the idea to search for King Arthur's tomb had taken hold at the abbey, and the monks went to work in earnest. In 1191, they claimed to have discovered Arthur's grave.

The story of the discovery is related by Giraldus Cambrensis (Gerald of Wales), a historian who visited the abbey soon afterward and met the abbot. Giraldus may be a reliable authority because he refused to accept much of the Arthurian legend and condemned Geoffrey of Monmouth for propagating the fancies that had appeared in the *History of the Kings of Britain.*

According to Giraldus, the monks at Glastonbury were given an indication of where to search by Henry II, who had been told by "an ancient Welsh bard, a singer of the past, that they would find the body at least sixteen feet beneath the earth, not in a tomb of stone, but in a hollow oak." It had been buried at such a depth "that it might not by any means be discovered by the Saxons, who occupied the island after his death, whom he had so often in his life defeated and almost utterly destroyed."

The monks roped off an area in the abbey grounds, erected a fence around it, and began to excavate. They had dug only a foot or two when a spade struck a slab of stone. Beneath the stone was a lead cross engraved with the Latin words:

HIC IACET SEPULTUS INCLYTUS REX ARTHURUS CUM WEN-NEVERIA UXORE SUA SECUNDA IN INSULA AVALLONIA

Here lies buried the renowned King Arthur with Guinevere his second wife in the Isle of Avalon

Excavating further, the monks unearthed a coffin made from a hollow oak trunk; inside they found the bones of a tall man at one end and those of a woman at the other. The skull of the woman was encircled by "a yellow tress of hair still retaining its colour and its freshness." But when a monk reached down to touch the hairs, they crumbled into dust.

The bones of the man were recovered less clumsily, and as each one appeared, the monks marveled at their size. His shin bone, Giraldus recounts, "when placed against that of the tallest man in the place, and planted in the earth near his foot, reached, as the Abbot showed us, a good three inches above his knee. And the skull was so large and capacious as to be a portent or a prodigy, for the eye-socket was a good palm in width. Moreover, there were ten wounds or more, all of which were scarred over, save one larger than the rest, which had made a great hole."

Arthur and Guinevere had been found at last. Now Glastonbury Abbey could be sure of an ongoing stream of visitors and pilgrims bearing gifts. New buildings slowly replaced those destroyed in the fire; a church that eventually would be the largest in England took its splendid shape, although the sprawling ruins of the abbey still may be seen. And in 1278, when King Edward I and Queen

Eleanor visited the abbey, the remains of Arthur and Guinevere were moved to a black marble tomb in the center of the choir and laid to rest. Two stone lions were placed at each end of the tomb, a statue of Arthur at the foot, and the lead cross found in the original tomb was placed above it.

The tomb remained undisturbed until the sixteenth century, when Henry VIII proclaimed the dissolution of all Britain's monasteries. The abbey's lands passed into private hands, and the buildings fell into ruins. In time, both the shrine and the original site of Arthur's grave were lost. In the eighteenth century, the lead cross, too, disappeared. The story of the monks' discovery was portrayed as a medieval fraud.

Certainly the lead cross did not date from the sixth century. A first-hand drawing made of it by a seventeenth-century historian shows a script of a much later date. In addition, the reference to Arthur as king indicates it was made long after his death at a time when his kingship had become part of the legend. It is impossible to be certain about the bones; they may have been those of an Iron Age man and woman, buried in a dugout canoe from the Glastonbury lake village after its destruction by the Belgae. The monks may have found them by chance while digging a grave, or they could have found them elsewhere and placed them in the spot most convenient for their discovery.

In addition, the Abbot of Glastonbury and his monks were not alone in wanting to make the discovery of Arthur's tomb. King Henry II was also interested, although he died before it was found. The people of Wales were in a state of rebellion. The legends of Arthur's survival were known to all Welshmen: There was real danger that a rebel leader might arouse widespread support by declaring that he was Arthur risen again to lead them against their Norman oppressors. It would be wise to offer proof to these descendants of the Britons that Arthur was dead.

Yet the monks' story is likely true. In 1934, an archaeological team digging in the abbey ruins came across the base of King Arthur's shrine, and in 1962, another team identified another grave the monks claimed to have dug up. It is possible that it was Arthur's grave and that it originally had been marked by the stone slab the monks discovered, but over the years had been covered by earth and lost to view. The cross could have been placed beneath the stone when the grave was marked as Arthur's in the tenth century when St. Dunstan was Abbot. Experts contend that its lettering could have been done then; the placing of lead crosses in graves was a common tenth-century practice.

This evidence makes the story more complicated, as other Glastonbury claims were quickly discredited. Geoffrey Ashe, a well-known writer on the Arthurian legend, has pointed out: "The bones of St. Patrick and St. Dunstan were denounced as spurious by indignant voices from Ireland and Canterbury. But the Welsh made no comment on the depressing exhumation of their national chief. They offered no alternative legend, they produced no counter-Avalon [indeed, no place in Britain other than Glastonbury ever has claimed to be the Isle of Avalon], such an acquiescent hush has its own eloquence. It hints at a longstanding tradition of Arthur's death and interment in the monastery, not widely familiar, but so fully accepted . . . that once the secret was out the English assertions could not be denied."

In any case, the 1962 discovery of the site of the grave, whether Arthur's or not, was the first of a series of archaeological finds that suggest that much more of the Arthurian legend may rest on fact than previously imagined.

6
UNEARTHING CAMELOT

The rediscovery in 1962 of the apparent site of Arthur's grave at Glastonbury led to renewed interest in the area of Somerset, and the persistent legend that the hill known as South Cadbury Castle, twelve miles southeast of Glastonbury, was once the famous Camelot.

In the early sixteenth century, the antiquarian John Leland visited the village of South Cadbury while touring England to gather information for his work, *History and Antiquities of this Nation*. The hill, the villagers told him, was "Camallate, sumtyme a famose toun or castelle." They had heard "say that Arture much resortid to Camalat." The top of the hill, where the ramparts of a centuries-old British hill fort could be traced beneath the grass, was known as Arthur's Palace, or so another antiquarian, William Camden, recorded when he visited Cadbury in Queen Elizabeth I's day. Within less than an hour's walk were two villages named Queen's Camel and West Camel. On the banks of the stream that wound through them, the battle of Camlann had been fought, where Mordred was slain and from which Arthur, seriously wounded, was carried to the Isle of Avalon at Glastonbury, a few miles away.

These local traditions have an undeniable air of authenticity. King Arthur's Causeway, which used to run across the marsh beneath the ramparts of the hill fort, is still visible along the fields of surrounding farms. The stream still winds through the fields between them, and hurried burials did take place in the past, indicating that a battle had been fought there. Over the centuries, plows turning up the ground of the eighteen-acre field on top of the summit uncovered a remarkable assortment of Roman coins, pottery, sling stones, building materials, and even traces of walls. It seemed that the hill, which had been occupied by Neolithic people more than 3,000 years before the birth of Christ, was still inhabited at the time of the Roman occupation of Britain. What archaeologists and antiquarians did not know, however, was if there ever had been an extensive reoccupation of the fort in the late fifth or early sixth century, the period in which Arthur must have lived.

In the 1890s, a party searching for evidence of such a reoccupation on the hill, an elderly man asked them if they had come to take away the sleeping king from the hollow hill. What that group found was not recorded, but a more rigorous excavation carried out shortly before World War I uncovered fragments of Romano-British pottery, along with artifacts featuring late Celtic workmanship. This was scarcely enough to establish a connection between South Cadbury Castle and Camelot.

In the 1950s, however, further discoveries were made, including pottery dating from the Neolithic period and the pre-Roman Iron Age. Most interesting from the Arthurian point of view were pottery fragments similar to some already unearthed at the Early Christian monastery at Tintagel in Cornwall, as well as other shards of what may be a Merovingian glass bowl imported from the Continent in the sixth century.

These discoveries were identified by Dr. Ralegh Radford, a British archaeologist, expert on Early Christian archaeology, and the most recent excavator of Glastonbury Abbey. Here was confirmation, Dr. Radford felt, "of the traditional identification of the site as the Camelot of Arthurian legend." Geoffrey Ashe, author of a number of articles and books on the Arthurian period and legend was also intrigued by the finds. But without large sums of money, no proper excavation could take place, and collecting sufficient funds seemed unlikely until 1965, when Radford and Ashe formed the Camelot Research Committee. Sir Mortimer Wheeler, the noted excavator of Mohenjo Daro and the Indus Valley of India, was appointed president of the committee, and the direction of the work was entrusted to Leslie Alcock, then Reader in Archaeology at the University College of South Wales. Newspapers, publishers, the British Broadcasting Corporation, universities, and private donors gave financial help. The excavations were not limited to discovering Camelot; they were devoted to unearthing all the secrets of the hill's history from its earliest known occupation by Neolithic peoples. The main focus was on finding archaeological proof of Arthur having lived there.

These hopes were increased by finds at Glastonbury Tor, the steep hill that rises above the ruins of the abbey, where fragments of amphorae were discovered, establishing that in the sixth century - Arthur's period - an important person had lived in Glastonbury Tor.

Philip Rahtz, director of excavations at Glastonbury, believes Glastonbury Tor may have been the stronghold of a local chieftain and perhaps a signal station of some kind. It could have been linked with South Cadbury Castle - the legendary Camelot - to the south, with Brent Knoll, at the western end of the Mendip Hills, to the north, and from Brent Knoll north across the mouth of the River Severn to another sixth-century British camp at Dinas Powys in South Wales. From Brent Knoll, both Cadbury Castle and Dinas Powys, some forty miles away, are visible. It is likely that cooperation and communication between the British on both sides of the Severn were very close in the sixth century. The Saxons didn't break through the line that connected the British defenders in Wales with those near South Cadbury Castle until the Battle of Dyrham in 577, sixty years after Arthur's fight at Mount Badon.

Extensive excavation at South Cadbury Castle began in the summer of 1966. The team of archaeologists and students who climbed the summit hoped to establish Arthur's existence, linking the hill with Camelot. Looking across the banks and ditches of the ramparts to the fields below, it was easy to imagine Arthur riding out from the misty swamps to do battle.

One volunteer said she believed Camelot was at South Cadbury. She felt sure that one day, she and her colleagues would come across the incontrovertible proof.

But the digging of 1966 revealed nothing as dramatic as a medallion bearing the imprint ARTORIUS. Perhaps it was unrealistic to hope for such clues: No one has ever found coins minted in Britain in the sixth century. But quite a few inscriptions from this period have been discovered in Britain and Ireland, incised on stone or metal. In Ireland and the Irish colonies in west Britain, these inscriptions are in Ogham, an alphabet of twenty letters, consisting of upright and sloping lines arranged in groups. In Britain, memorial slabs and pillars are engraved in the Roman fashion, although these are usually found only in consecrated Early Christian cemeteries.

No inscriptions of any kind, however, turned up at South Cadbury in 1966. But the short and preliminary excavations were illuminating.

The researchers found a stone wall built by Saxons that likely protected a fortified burh, or settlement. This lent weight to the belief that eleventh-century coins bearing the mark CADANBYRIG, which have been discovered elsewhere, were made at a mint at South Cadbury. The archaeologists also found pieces of Roman armor, a pre-Roman Iron-Age trench, the remains of a collapsed Iron Age house, and from the Early Christian period between Roman times and the age of the English mint, shards of Mediterranean wine jugs and dishes, suggesting some occupation in the sixth century. "This brief reconnaissance," concluded the report by Leslie Alcock, "covered less than one seven-hundredth part of the interior and has amply confirmed the rich potential of South Cadbury Castle in both structural and cultural terms. Particular interest attaches to the . . . long perspective of Celtic and Romano-British occupation which forms the chronological background to the Arthurian period at Cadbury. Clearly the site, in all its aspects, now demands large-scale exploration."

In the summer of 1967, excavations began again, after the Camelot Research Committee's appeal for funds had brought in further contributions. That year, they made more discoveries. The Saxon wall, with twenty-four feet of it unearthed, was the longest seen in England. Beneath it was the last Iron Age rampart, and between the two was what the excavators called the Stony Bank.

The Stony Bank contained yet another shard of imported sixth-century pottery, fragments of Roman-style roof tiles, lumps of tufa - a light stone used by Romans as a building material - and a Roman sling stone. The sling stone's presence showed that this layer of the wall must have been constructed after the Roman conquest of Britain; the tiles and lumps of tufa likely came from a pagan temple built in the third or fourth century. The remains of such temples already had been discovered in other Iron-Age forts in Britain. The pottery presumably got there after the Stony Bank was built and before the Saxon wall was erected. Thanks to these discoveries, it's clear that Cadbury Castle was re-fortified in the sixth century as a stronghold against the Saxon invaders.

Prior to digging out the wall and new section of the summit the researchers conducted a geophysical survey. Instruments that looked something like mine-detectors scanned the pattern, shape, and density of the archaeological features beneath the turf. These instruments, known as soil conductivity meters, work on a principle similar to radar. They had not been used in archaeological work before and were successful in helping Alcock decide which areas were the most promising for that year's digging. When printed, the readings revealed traces of what might have been extensive buildings constructed on top of the old Iron-Age fortress of Arthur's time. Something that looked remarkably like a main hall aroused excitement among the researchers.

Subsequent excavations did not live up to the promise of the conductivity meters, but they did uncover something that baffled experts. As the weeks of July and August 1967 passed, the archaeologists unearthed a trench that followed no explicable pattern.

None of the experts on hand could explain what purpose this zig-zagging trench might serve. At first, they thought the hill had been used for military exercises during World War I. Volunteers shared their interpretations: "A giraffe's tomb" and "Patio of King Arthur's Palace."

Then, someone realized that if the U-shaped part of the pattern were repeated beneath the turf outside the area of excavation, the combined trenches would form a cross.

A look at the geophysical survey plan showed that the pattern did, indeed, suggest that a cruciform trench might be in that sector of the hill. No one, however, had been looking for such a shape. The team had been seeking evidence of the round buildings of the Iron Age and the rectangular buildings of the Early Christian period.

Alcock ordered three trial digs outside the excavated area. In each case, the excavators uncovered a further section of the trench. The cruciform plan was established.

This design could be explained most easily as the plan of a church. Such a plan, in the shape of an equal-armed Greek cross, first appeared in the Middle East in the late fifth century. It was by no means common, however, in Arthur's time. Some historians have suggested that this could have been Arthur's chapel at Camelot, later demolished by the Saxons to provide stones for their wall. But no traces of mortar or stone chips have been found to confirm this hypothesis, and it seems more likely that work on the building was abandoned as soon as its foundations were in place.

Experts question whether the trench was dug in the sixth century, or even by the Saxons; the unfinished foundation may have been laid as late as the eleventh century, and the building may have been broken off when the mint was removed and the Saxon settlement abandoned early in the reign of King Canute. But carbon-dating by British archaeologists in 2012 suggested that clay crucibles and vivid blue-green window glass, uncovered at the site in the 1950s, were made circa 680. That puts the structure within the reign of King Ine of Wessex, who was credited in *The Anglo-Saxon Chronicle* with building a monastery at Glastonbury. The remains of five glassworks at the site also provide the earliest and most substantial evidence of glass-making in Saxon Britain.

Excavation at South Cadbury Castle resumed in the summer of 1968, and further Arthurian evidence was unearthed, including fine fragments of sixth-century wine jugs; traces of what may prove to be the Saxon entrance to the stronghold, the "gate of Camelot"; and part of the foundation trench for what appears to be a large, sixth-century hall cut into the bedrock of the plateau. This building, thirty-five by seventy feet, may have been the great hall of Camelot, but its discovery marked an exciting moment in the search for King Arthur's Britain.

A hundred miles from Glastonbury, the ruins of Tintagel Castle emerge from a rocky peninsula overlooking the Celtic Sea, the part of the Atlantic Ocean that laps at the south coast of Ireland. The place of Arthur's conception, if not his birth, the castle yielded another fragment of Arthurian history. Tintagel's association with Arthur began in the twelfth century with Geoffrey of Monmouth. When excavation of the site began in the 1930s, many historians were quick to quell public excitement over the possibility that it may lead to some historical evidence of Arthur's existence. Archaeologist Ralegh Radford declared that "No concrete evidence whatsoever has yet been found to support the legendary connection of the Castle with King Arthur." But others were not so dismissive. In 1998, the discovery of a sixth-century stone carving sparked the imaginations of Arthurian scholars.

The artifact, which has become known as the Artognou Stone, is believed to have originated as a dedication stone for some building or structure, and later broken into two pieces, one of which was reused as part of a drain. The dating of the stone was due to its proximity to fifth- and sixth-century pottery excavated nearby, and the formation of its inscriptions, which are from that period. The top right-hand corner of the stone features a diagonal cross, bordered by letters on both sides. One of the letters is worn away. The other is an "A." Below is the inscription, "PATTERN[-] COLI AVI FICIT ARTOGNOU," which is translated as "Artognou descendant of Pattern[us] Colus made (this)." Some have suggested that Artognou is a variant of Arthur, though others see it as only a passing resemblance. Artognou, in Old Breton, literally means "Bear Knowing."

Whether fact or fantasy, the Artognou Stone has drawn large numbers of both scholars and believers in the legend to Tintagel Castle. In 2010, 190,000 people visited the site. Some have suggested that St. Nectan's Kieve, a pool beneath a waterfall on the Trevillet River, is where Arthur and his Knights of the Round Table were anointed before embarking on their quest for the Holy Grail.

A footpath connects Tintagel Castle with the hill reputed to have once held Camelot and King Arthur's court. Known as Arthur's Way, it is walked by thousands who believe that their steps trace those once taken by those men of legend.

7

UNMISTAKABLE TRUTHS

Even if the excavations at South Cadbury fail to uncover the reality of the Once and Future King, they have dispelled the illusion that Arthur was the magical king of medieval romance. We can imagine him now, not as a monarch clad in gleaming armor parading through the stone halls, particolored pavilions, and painted towers of medieval Camelot, but as a stern warrior facing brutal sixth-century warfare, living in a stronghold built for defense rather than pleasure.

He does not wear a silver breastplate, but a leather cuirass; not a plumed helmet, but a close-fitting iron headpiece lined with leather. His breeches and boots are brown leather and his red woolen cloak, the only splash of color in an otherwise drab appearance, is fastened at his right shoulder with a bronze brooch of Celtic design. At his left side, he carries an iron sword in a leather scabbard; in his right hand he grasps the wooden shaft of an iron spear.

With this picture of Arthur in mind, the fanciful legends first appearing in the pages of Malory seem to contain a kernel of truth. Undeniably, a truth buried deep within a legend is nothing new, and in this connection the story of German archaeologist Heinrich Schliemann is much to the point.

As a boy in the 1830s, Schliemann was fond of fables and legends. In particular, he loved the epic stories of Homer's heroes, Achilles and Hector, Paris and Helen, and the city of Troy, capital of King Priam, which, after a ten-year siege by the Greeks, was captured, burned, and leveled. All his life Schliemann remembered a book about the Trojan War and the adventures of Odysseus that his father gave him when he was ten years old. He decided when he was grown up, he would go to Troy and excavate the legendary city.

Schliemann left school at fourteen and worked for five-and-a-half years in a grocery store, then became an office boy in Amsterdam and spent his spare time studying foreign languages, becoming fluent in Dutch, English, French, Italian, Portuguese, and Spanish. He learned Russian to represent his company in St. Petersburg, and did so well there that he soon was in business on his own as an import-export merchant. He retired in 1863 at the age of forty-five and devoted himself to the mythical studies that captured his imagination as a child.

In 1868, he sailed for Greece, determined to prove that the scholars and experts who had relegated the Trojan epic to the world of fiction were wrong. He was as convinced - as he had been as a boy - that the Greece of Homer's *Iliad* existed, that Achilles and Agamemnon, Hector and Aeneas, were heroes who had lived and fought and died. Again and again, Schliemann read the *Iliad*, searching for clues that would lead him to Troy, following Homer's directions as best he could. His trail led him to Hissarlik, a small town in western Turkey. There, ignoring ridicule and discomfort, Schliemann set 100 men to work digging. They uncovered the ruins of Priam's city and traces of a civilization previously unknown to archaeology.

Schliemann's faith and ability proved a legend can have its base in historical reality. So may it be some day with Camelot and the Arthurian legend. In the 1970s, English writer Beram Saklatvala made several suggestions to account for some of the legend's varied details. He guessed that the source of the French book from which Malory claimed he had taken the story of the sword in the stone might have been a lost Latin chronicle in which this sentence or something similar appeared: "Arthur gladium ex saxo eripuit" – "Arthur drew, or seized, a sword from the stone." This remarkable feat, Malory tells us, was beyond the power of other men and proved Arthur was the rightful king. This story and others like it induced Caxton to tell his readers that they were "at liberty to believe" *Le Morte d'Arthur* was not all true. But Saklatvala suggests the Latin phrase might be a mistaken copy of the record of an authentic fact.

The words that arouse disbelief are *ex saxo*, "from a stone." Medieval clerks often omitted the letter "n" and showed the omission by a stroke drawn in above the next letter, so that ex saxoē, or ex saxone, would mean that Arthur took the sword from the Saxon rather than from the stone. Whether we are to interpret it that Arthur struck the sword from the hand of a much-feared Saxon warrior in combat, or that the Saxon is intended to mean the Saxon race whose ambitions were thwarted at Mount Badon, it is not hard to believe that such a victory would ensure Arthur the leadership of the British armies, if not the throne of the British kingdom in the West Country.

Saklatvala argues that the story of the other sword in the legend, Excalibur, may have passed into the realm of myth by a similar process. In Malory's version of the tale, the sword appears in the midst of a lake of "fair water and broad," and after the battle of Camlann, when Arthur instructs Sir Bedivere to return it to the waters, "there came an arm above the water and met it, and caught it, and so shook it thrice and brandished, and then vanished away the hand with the sword in the water." Geoffrey of Monmouth also writes of Arthur's "peerless sword, forged in the Isle of Avalon," which he calls Caliburn.

Saklatvala suggests an early chronicle showed Arthur obtaining his sword *ex cale burno* beside the river Cale, in which case its name and its connection with water would be readily explained. The Romans ascribed some of the merits of their swords to the quality of the water into which the blacksmith plunged the heated blades in order to temper them. The river Cale is within an hour's ride of South Cadbury Castle.

Some scholars have refuted Saklatvala's thesis. Apart from the fact that the medieval Latin word burna, "stream," is recorded for the first time only around 1135, when Geoffrey was completing his *History*, the Somersetshire river Cale in his day was written Cawel; the spelling "Cale" does not appear until Elizabethan days. There is also doubt about whether the ex in Excalibur stands for the Latin word meaning "out of" or if it is just a prefix used to accentuate the first syllable as in the Old French form of the word "escalibor" - like that in "especial," compared with "special."

The generally accepted derivation of the name of Arthur's sword, according to Arthurian scholar R. S. Loomis, is Celtic rather than Latin. Excalibur's name in the Welsh romances is Caledvwlch, based on the Welsh words calet, "hard," and bwlch, "notch." Loomis believed this was just a Welsh approximation of the name of another famous sword, renowned in Irish legends: Caladbolg, meaning "Hard Sword" or "Hard Sheath," which was made by the fairies for an Ulster hero named Fergus. In one of these Irish sagas, the hero Fergus Mac Leite uses Caladbolg to do battle with a lake monster. Victorious, but mortally wounded, he begs his followers to give his sword only to another hero named Fergus, and to treasure it "that none other take it from you; my share of the matter for all time shall be this: that men shall rehearse the story of the sword." There are obvious parallels here with Mallory's story of Arthur, although no scholar has done more than point out the similarities.

The fact that the quest for Excalibur's source leads back to Celtic myth is not surprising. It was natural that the defeated British people should imbue their greatest hero with legendary attributes that originally belonged to other heroes, or even gods. As Loomis put it: "Throughout the world's history, clouds of legend have gathered about the heads of military leaders who have caught the imagination of a people. This happened to Alexander and Charlemagne, to Napoleon and Washington. For the Britons it was enough that Arthur inflicted a series of defeats on their heathen foes and staved off for a time their expulsion from what was to be England. . . . To this racial hero the Welsh and to some extent the Cornish attached a floating mass of native traditions, together with matter derived from Ireland and the Britons of the North. This they passed on to the Bretons, who shared their passionate devotion to the memory of Arthur, and the Bretons in turn, speaking French, were able by the fire and the charm of their recitals to captivate the imagination of the non-Celtic peoples. Thus, the obscure battle leader of a defeated race became the champion of all Christendom, his knights paragons of valor and chivalry, and the ladies of his court nonpareils of beauty."

The legends attribute other weapons to Arthur as well, some whose origins and utility are more practical than Excalibur. At the Battle of Mount Badon, Arthur is said to have wielded a spear called Rhongomyniad, which translates to "spear, striker, slayer." Another legend has Arthur slaying a witch with a dagger called Carnwennan, meaning "little white hilt." And the sword with which Mordred killed Arthur at the Battle of Camlann was called Clarent – a sword of peace meant for knighting ceremonies, stolen by Arthur's illegitimate son.

But there is no need to find historical parallels to believe in the reality of Arthur. We may believe nothing else in *Le Morte d'Arthur*, but the existence of its central figure is scarcely in doubt. We even may believe, as one historian said of the Glastonbury stories, that none of the Arthurian legends bears any relation to recorded facts, but the existence of those legends is in itself a fact.

Even now, after 1,500 years, new evidence could dispel the mists of legend and reveal an undeniable truth. Until then, we can piece together a biography of Arthur.

He was born around 475 into a well-to-do West Country family and given a Roman name, Artorius, in token of the family's traditional loyalty to the empire. As a young man in the Christian kingdom of Ambrosius, the last Roman outpost in Britain, he showed a talent for leadership. He assumed responsibility for the defense of the kingdom on Ambrosius' death. He formed and trained an effective cavalry, which fought in the traditional Roman style. He persuaded most of the British kings to accept him as their leader, a Count of Britain on the Roman model, and to appoint him commander.

With his own cavalry and whatever support he could gather, he traveled throughout Britain, attacking invaders in campaigns that took him from Chester in the west to the forests of Caledonia north of Hadrian's Wall, and into lands occupied by the East Saxons and the North Angles. He gave his cause a Christian and Catholic tenor by invoking the protection of the Virgin Mary, yet he offended the Catholic Church by forcibly taking supplies from monasteries.

In 516, his enemies converged upon his defenses in the southwest, but at Mount Badon, somewhere near the Wansdyke, he led his cavalry against them, inflicting such an overwhelming defeat that peace reigned for fifty years. That peace was broken by a civil war in which Arthur and Mordred, the illegitimate son who sought to replace him, both were killed. For some twenty years, however, Arthur had been the recognized master of those parts of Britain not occupied by the Angles and Saxons. He was proclaimed king by his troops, and he held with his knights a court that later generations were to know as Camelot.

Once again, facts and speculations merge into myth, and we are left searching for that incontestable proof that someday may solve the riddle of Malory's "great conqueror and excellent King." He has meant something different to each generation: To one, he is a tyrant king; to another, a mighty warrior; to yet another, a ruler of a magical subterranean kingdom; to Malory, he is a hero, noble and tragic, and it is this image that has left the most lasting impression.

Yet even while Malory wrote, the temper of the times had changed. The world he described still had its appeal, even to Henry VIII, who boasted of his descent from Arthur through the Welsh princes to whom the Tudor family were distantly related and enjoyed jousts, tournaments, and sport of all kinds. But Henry was exemplar of knightly behavior, and in the upsurge of interest in classical literature and art, and the clash between Protestant and Catholic faiths that characterized the sixteenth century, the idea of medieval chivalry began to seem an anachronism. It was not just that new weapons had rendered knights obsolete; the practical and realistic Elizabethans tended to see them in terms of Cervantes' Don Quixote, tilting at windmills.

Some Elizabethans could - among them Edmund Spenser, whose *The Faerie Queene*, published at the end of the sixteenth century, combined the influences of the Renaissance with the antique legends of Britain. Spenser died without completing his work, but in a 1589 letter to Sir Walter Raleigh, he described his intentions: "to fashion a gentleman or noble person in vertuous and gentle discipline. Which for that I conceived should be the most plausible and pleasing . . . I chose the historie of king Arthure, as most fit for the excellencie of his person, beeing made famous by many mens former workes, and also furthest from the danger of envie, and suspicion of present time." Following the style of Homer, Vergil, and the Italian poets Ariosto and Tasso, Spenser has labored to portray in Arthur "before he was king, the image of a brave knight, perfected in the twelve private morall vertues, as Aristotle hath devised."

Despite Spenser's intention of making Arthur the hero of his work, the prince is more an incidental figure in the six books of *The Faerie Queene*; he plays no significant part in the adventures of the various knights and ladies. Spenser uses material from Geoffrey of Monmouth's *History*, adapting or altering it to suit his purposes. He treats Arthur as a legendary figure rather than an historical one, an attitude that foreshadows that of many writers of the following century.

"Charles James Stuart Claims Arthur's Seat" was a popular slogan at the coronation of James I in 1603. As the Stuart king of Scotland ascended the throne of England, poets boasted that, with Britain united under one crown, the prophecies of Merlin were fulfilled. Ben Jonson and Thomas Campion wrote masques and pageants celebrating James' accession; Jonson planned an Arthurian epic. As the new monarch entered London, a complicated double British pedigree, claiming James' direct descent from Arthur on both sides of his family, was displayed on two seventy-foot pyramids at the entrance to the Strand.

But the Arthurian golden age was a short one. James and his son Charles I believed they were divinely appointed to rule; Parliament, increasing in strength, grew more rebellious. The Stuart kings were poor representatives of the royal state, and those favoring Parliament and the English constitution began to scorn their ancestor, King Arthur, and look instead to Arthur's ancient enemies, the Anglo-Saxons, as the real fathers of the country, language, and laws. Geoffrey of Monmouth's *History* was ridiculed; he had, according to one observer, "stuft himselfe with infinit Fables and grosse absurdities," scoffed one Parliamentary sympathizer.

The poet Milton, fascinated by Italian romances and influenced by Spenser, planned an epic poem on "the kings of my native land, and Arthur, who carried war even into fairyland." Later, as a staunch Puritan and supporter of Parliament, he not only abandoned Arthur as a subject for an epic but also, in his *History of Britain*, made every attempt to discredit the British hero, calling him "more renown'd in Songs and Romances, than in True stories." Nennius he dismisses as "a very trivial writer," and after a discussion of the Battle of Mount Badon, Milton sums up: "But who Arthur was, and whether ever any such reign'd in Britan, hath bin doubted heertofore, and may again with good reason."

But after the Civil War and the bleak rule of Oliver Cromwell came the Restoration of Charles II in 1660, and the first new book on Arthur in many decades. John Dryden, a loyalist, wanted to produce an Arthurian epic poem that would popularize Stuart rule but was too busy writing plays to compose it. In 1691, he used the subject for an opera for which Henry Purcell supplied the music. This concentrates primarily on Arthur's battles with the Saxons and makes Arthur and a Saxon prince rivals for the love of Emmeline, the blind daughter of the Duke of Cornwall. Arthur wins his bride, whose sight is restored by magic drops provided by Merlin.

It is ironic that the three greatest poets of the seventeenth century, Jonson, Milton, and Dryden planned epic poems on the subject of Arthur, but did not write them. Two massive Arthurian epics were composed, however, by King William III's physician, Sir Richard Blackmore, who found the writing of epics "an Innocent Amusement to entertain me in such leisure hours which were usually past away before in Conversation and unprofitable hearing and telling of News." He would have done better to confine himself to the news; he and his epics are known today only because a far better poet, Alexander Pope, labeled him "the everlasting Blackmore" who "sings so loudly and who sings so long."

The eighteenth century saw little interest in Arthur. Merlin had become a figure of mockery; astrologers used images of his head on the signs outside their fortune-telling establishments. The popular tale of Tom Thumb made the tiny man a knight at King Arthur's court, in love with the king's daughter Princess Hunca Munca. It was not until the end of the century that a rekindled interest in the Middle Ages brought Romantic poets and painters once again to the Arthurian cycle. Early in the nineteenth century, Walter Scott and Robert Southey wrote of Arthur and proposed or edited updated versions of Malory. By the middle of the century, medievalism was reflected in the Gothic art and architecture of Victorian England. Edward Bulwer-Lytton, William Morris, and the Pre-Raphaelite Brotherhood of artists and writers and various lesser poets turned their attention to the Arthurian theme. And in 1859, Alfred Tennyson published the first series of the *Idylls of the King*, which translated Malory's characters into a gospel for Victorian times.

Tennyson contemplated this project for years and had visited places associated with Arthur in the West Country, seeking material and impressions. He read and reread *Le Morte d'Arthur* and studied the French and Norman chronicles and the legends of Wales. He published his first Arthurian poem, "The Lady of Shalott" in 1832, when he was twenty-three; he was planning an epic work on what he called "the greatest of all poetic subjects." But he was uncertain of what shape his piece should take. By the 1850s, he had found the ideal narrative: a series of verses that described the interval between Arthur's birth and his disappearance into the mists of Avalon.

Publication of the first four idylls in 1859 was greeted with unparalleled enthusiasm; 10,000 copies sold within the first week, and Tennyson was offered 5,000 guineas for another volume of the same length. Over the next twenty-five years he wrote further idylls about Arthur, his knights, and the ladies of his court. The public was enthralled; at one point, Tennyson's publishers had to contend with orders for 40,000 copies of an edition prior to publication.

Tennyson's Arthur, a "blameless King" of utmost moral rectitude, is far removed from Malory's passionate knight. In the *Idylls,* there is none of the amorous environment that pervades Malory's Camelot. Just as Geoffrey of Monmouth's Arthur was called forth in Stephen's time to give a heroic British origin to the Norman kingdom, Tennyson's Arthur reflects the sentiments and morality admired by Queen Victoria and Prince Albert. The poet depicts Britain of Arthur's day not as an ideal period, but as an analogy from which Victorian readers could draw parallels for their own time. He stressed idealism, chivalry, unselfish patriotism, and religious faith, and attempted to show that even the finest ideals are subject to defeat. In the end, his message was one of hope, as Bedivere, despairing, calls the "true old times ... dead,/When every morning brought a noble chance,/And every chance brought out a noble knight."

> And slowly answer'd Arthur from the barge:
> "The old order changeth, yielding place to
> new, And God fulfils himself in many ways,
> Lest one good custom should corrupt the
> world. Comfort thyself: what comfort is in
> me? I have lived my life, and that which I
> have done May He within Himself make
> pure! but thou, If thou shouldst never see
> my face again, Pray for my soul. More
> things are wrought by prayer Than this
> world dreams of . . ."

The idealism of Tennyson's Arthur has been seen as a reflection of Prince Albert, to whom, after his premature death in 1861, Tennyson dedicated the *Idylls*: "These to His Memory - since he held them dear/Perchance as finding there unconsciously/ Some image of himself." The dedication certainly makes the epic a public compliment to his royal patrons, but his purpose went deeper than that. The characters are symbolic: Arthur represents the soul, struggling to fulfill itself in the world (represented by marriage with Guinevere), while the Round Table stands for the soul's attempt to ennoble and control human emotions - an ideal that is corrupted and eroded by the sin of Lancelot and Guinevere. But as Tennyson put it: "Every reader must find his own interpretation according to his ability, and according to his sympathy with the poet."

The influence of Arthurian legend upon the art and literature of the period continued; photography, then a new technology, was employed to make a series of illustrations for Tennyson's *Idylls*, while some of the finest artists of the day contributed their visions of Arthur's world. Musicians, too, were drawn to the story of Arthur, notably German composer Richard Wagner, who produced the first of his Arthurian music-dramas, Lohengrin, in 1850 and followed it with the famous Tristan und Isolde in 1865 and in 1882 with Parsifal, based upon legends of Percival and the quest for the Holy Grail. The regular performance of Wagner's works and their overwhelming popularity formed yet another current in the spread of Arthurian influences.

In 1958, the concept of knighthood was celebrated anew with T. H. White's books about Arthur, which he gathered together under the title *The Once and Future King*, which brought the legend to life for a new generation through Camelot, the musical and the film based upon them.

White presents the story in a vivid light, filling it with humor and magic, with lessons in hawking and boar-hunting, archery and jousting, history and animal lore. But he treats his material with the same respect as Malory, and at the end of the last book, White brings Malory into the story as an innocent-faced page. Arthur, tired and soon to die, tells the boy what the purpose of his life has been and urges him not to fight in the final battle with Mordred on the following day, but to take his horse to Warwickshire to carry on the idea of the Round Table and spread its message to future generations: "Put it like this. There was a king once, called King Arthur. That is me. When he came to the throne of England, he found that all the kings and barons were fighting against each other like madmen. . . . They did a lot of bad things, because they lived by force. Now this king had an idea, and the idea was that force ought to be used, if it were used at all, on behalf of justice, not on its own account. Follow this, young boy. He thought that if he could get his barons fighting for truth, and to help weak people, and to redress wrongs, then their fighting might not be such a bad thing as once it used to be. So he gathered together all the true and kindly people that he knew, and he dressed them in armour, and he made them knights, and taught them his idea, and set them down, at a Round Table. And King Arthur loved his Table with all his heart. He was prouder of it than he was of his own dear wife, and for many years his new knights went about killing ogres, and rescuing damsels and saving poor prisoners, and trying to set the world to rights. That was the King's idea."

And that, to White, was what mattered most.

He was not concerned with the real Arthur; he turned history upside-down to recreate a medieval knight at odds with the ways of a violent world. He despised historians and archaeologists who were trying to track a legend to its historical roots and, in his view, destroy its beauty. For him, Arthur was "not a distressed Briton hopping about in a suit" of armor in the fifth century," but a true knight with "an open face, with kind eyes and a reliable or faithful expression, as though he was a good learner who enjoyed being alive. . . . He had never been unjustly treated, for one thing, so he was kind to other people."

8
LOVE, LEGEND, AND LEGACY

Arthur is clearly the ruler of his own legend, but he doesn't stand alone. His character is forged in the fires of conflict, passion, and friendship. His court exhibits all the intricacies of courage and cowardice, loyalty and betrayal, magic and might. The Arthur we know would not have been the same without the sorcery of Merlin, the love of Guinevere, or the treachery of Mordred. This is where we leave the legend.

All the essential elements of a classic hero story are present in the Arthur legend, which has perhaps been the secret to its endurance. Throughout history, myth and folklore around the world have shared the same basic structure: the hero's quest becomes a symbol of humanity's search for harmony and a personal journey toward enlightenment. But if Arthur was, indeed, more than a symbol, the key players of his story must also have some foundation in fact. From cave painters to Hollywood screenwriters, storytellers have always exaggerated the stories of their heroes. Historical threads become so interwoven with fantasy it's nearly impossible to separate fact from fiction or to distinguish real people from imaginary characters.

Before Arthur, there was Merlin, who, according to legend, orchestrated the birth of the Once and Future King. The prevailing image of Merlin is of a gray-bearded wizard, dressed in robes and hooded cloaks. In Geoffrey of Monmouth's *History of the Kings of Britain*, Merlin entered Arthurian legend as a prophetic youth; in Geoffrey's *Prophetiae Merlini* (*Prophecies of Merlin*) – his earliest surviving work - the text is purported to be the wizard's actual words. This is telling, in that many of the prophecies in this book are said to have originated with sixth-century prophet and madman Myrddin Wyllt.

Born around 540, Myrddin Wyllt, also known as Lailoken, was an adviser to Gwenddoleu, a Celtic king who ruled an area of England now known as Arthuret. Gwenddoleu was a descendant of Coel Hen, the progenitor of several royal lines and possibly the historical basis for the nursery rhyme "Old King Cole." In 573, Gwenddoleu and Myrddin were waged in the Battle of Arfderydd, which pitted several allied armies against each other. When the king was killed, his adviser went mad and fled into the Caledonian Forest, where he lived among the animals and discovered his gift of prophecy.

A fifteenth-century Latin manuscript tells of encounters between Saint Kentigern – also known as St. Mungo, the patron saint and founder of the Scotland city of Glasgow – and a "naked, hairy madman who is called Lailoken, although said by some to be called Merlynum or Merlin, who declares that he has been condemned for his sins to wander in the company of beasts." Myrddin appears again later in the story to ask Saint Kentigern to administer to him the holy Sacrament, claiming to have seen a vision of his own death. First, he stated, "I shall be stoned and die by clubs;" then, "my body will be pierced by a sharp stake, and thus will my spirit fall;" and finally, "I shall be sunk in water and so end my life on earth." Kentigern was reluctant to trust Myrddin, "for he never said the same things twice but made indirect and conflicting predictions." Still, the saint was persuaded to carry out his wishes. Later that day, according to the legend, the prophet was captured by a king's shepherd, who beat him with clubs and cast him into the river Tweed.

The *Prophecies of Merlin*, which introduced a new, distinctly English style of political philosophy called Galifridian, was widely read and almost universally believed in the early to mid-1130s. References to recent historical events – such as the sinking of the White Ship, which drowned the only surviving legitimate son of England's King Henry I in 1120 – were believed to have been uttered by a prophet nearly six centuries before they occurred.

Geoffrey used passages from the *Prophecies* for use in the *History of the Kings of Britain*. In one, Merlin is consulted by Vortigern, a British warlord who is trying to build a tower, only to have it collapse each time it is completed. Merlin discovers the reason behind its unsteady foundation: Beneath it was a lake, in which two dragons, one white and one red, were battling. The wizard saw the dragons as representative of the war between the Saxons and the Britons, and foresaw its conclusion: "Woe to the red dragon, for his banishment hasteneth on. His lurking holes shall be seized by the white dragon, which signifies the Saxons whom you invited over; but the red denotes the British nation, which shall be oppressed by the white. Therefore shall its mountains be leveled as the valleys, and the rivers of the valleys shall run with blood. The exercise of religion shall be destroyed, and churches be laid open to ruin. At last the oppressed shall prevail, and oppose the cruelty of foreigners. For a boar of Cornwall shall give his assistance, and trample their necks under his feet. The islands of the ocean shall be subject to his power, and he shall possess the forests of Gaul. The house of Romulus shall dread his courage, and his end shall be doubtful. He shall be celebrated in the mouths of the people and his exploits shall be food to those that relate them."

The Boar of Cornwall is a reference to Arthur. But the legend of the two dragons was first told about Aurelius Ambrosius, a character in Nennius' *Historia Brittonum* based on a fifth-century Romano-British war leader named Ambrosius Aurelianus, who won an important battle against the Saxons. This suggests that the Merlin of legend was actually an amalgam of Myrddin Wyllt and Ambrosius Aurelianus, though there are distinctions between the two. Most significantly, while Ambrosius is the son of a Roman consul, Merlin was sired by a demon who laid with a king's daughter. In Geoffrey's *History*, Merlin is also credited with creating Stonehenge as a burial place for Ambrosius Aurelianus. But the wizard's bargain with Uther Pendragon at Tintagel, which produced Arthur, is his crowning achievement. Though Malory's *Le Morte d'Arthur* has Merlin return to raise and tutor Arthur, Geoffrey makes no mention of him after Arthur's birth.

Like Merlin, there is evidence Arthur's legendary Queen Guinevere combined traits and tales told of more than one person. She first appears in an eleventh-century Welsh tale, *Culhwch and Olwen*, but is only mentioned as Arthur's queen. In or about 1136, a Welsh cleric named Caradoc of Llancarfan, writing about the life of sixth-century British monk St. Gildas, introduces Guinevere as a damsel in distress. In *Life of Gildas*, the queen is abducted and held prisoner at Glastonbury by a villain named Melwas, "king of the Summer Country." Arthur searches for his lost love for a year, then assembles his knights to storm Melwas's impenetrable castle to retrieve her. In later versions of the story, Melwas is called Maleagant, and Guinevere's savior is Lancelot. The abduction and rescue of Guinevere is a common theme in the tales of King Arthur.

A collection of Welsh manuscripts, *Trioedd Ynys Prydein (Triads of the Island of Britain*, or the *Welsh Triads*), suggests that Arthur had three wives, all named Guinevere. His first wife, according to these texts, was the daughter of Cywryd of Gwent, a Welsh kingdom lying between the Wye and Usk rivers. This Guinevere was sent by her father to a Roman camp on the east bank of the Nith River to be trained as a warrior and to command an army, where she supposedly met Arthur. A sturdy woman with long, golden hair and blue eyes, she was pined after by many men but promised in marriage to one of her father's rivals, King Urien of Gorre. When Guinevere broke off her betrothal to marry Arthur, a war ensued between the kings that spanned four battles – all won by Arthur.

In one version of the story, Urien is the father of Maleagant, and orchestrates the abduction of Guinevere. In another, Urien marries Arthur's half-sister, the dark sorceress Morgan le Fay, sister of Morgause. Abducted a second time by Urien, Guinevere is thrown into a pit of vipers and fatally bitten on the finger. Her body is then retrieved and buried at Avalon.

Arthur married a second Guinevere, this one the daughter of Gwythyr ap Greidawl, a knight in Arthur's court. This Guinevere had a sister, Gwenhwyfach, who tricked Arthur into believing she was her sister for two and a half years before the deception was uncovered. Enmity between the sisters may have also led to the Battle of Camlann, in which Arthur was mortally wounded. The *Welsh Triads* refers to a slap that Gwenhwyfach dealt Guinevere as one of the "Three Harmful Blows of the Island of Britain."

The *Triads* list Arthur's third wife Guinevere as the daughter of a giant named Gogfran Gawr. On the frontier of Shropshire, west of Wales, there was a land of giants called Bronn Wrgan. In one story, Gogfran had imprisoned some brothers of Guinevere there, and Arthur was sent to rescue them. Arthur cut off the head of the largest giant, tossed it into the middle of the River Teme, and used it as a stepping stone to get to Knucklas Castle, where he married Guinevere.

The Guinevere of Malory's *Le Morte d'Arthur* is likely a combination of all three women. In this and other non-Welsh medieval romances, she is the daughter of King Leodegrance, who served under Arthur's biological father, Uther Pendragon. When Uther died, his Round Table was entrusted to Leodegrance; later it was returned to Arthur as a wedding present. Leodegrance was one of the few kings who accepted Arthur as overlord, making his kingdom a target of a rebel ruler named Rience. Notorious for trimming his robe with the beards of eleven kings he had conquered, Rience is determined to make Arthur's beard the twelfth. Arthur comes to Leodegrance's aid, thwarting an invasion by Rience, and meeting Guinevere for the first time.

Both early and later Arthurian legend endow Arthur with sons, at least four of whom were assumed to have been born to Guinevere. The most notable exception is Mordred, the son of Arthur and his half-sister Morgause, who, according to prophecy, kills his father the king. Another affair with a woman named Eleirch produced a son, Cydfan. His four sons with Guinevere - Anir, Gwydre, Llacheu, and Duran – all met untimely deaths, killed in battle or through treachery. A sixteenth-century British romance writer, Richard Johnson, ascribed another illegitimate son to Arthur – Tom, who bore him grandsons, referred to only as the Black Knight and the Faerie Knight.

Guinevere's increasing importance in the Arthurian legend parallels women's emergence, over the centuries, from an inferior role. In the early tales, Guinevere was little more than Arthur's chattel, notable only for her beauty. By the twelfth century, however, she had become the heroine of a courtly love affair with Lancelot, the noblest of Arthur's knights, whose reverence for her naturally increased her status.

As each generation of storytellers and artists has retold the Arthurian legend, emphases have shifted, and fresh heroes have been given prominence. But Lancelot has been the most famous of Arthur's knights since the twelfth century, when Countess Marie de Champagne commissioned a romance glorifying courtly love, with Lancelot as its hero. The French poem - *Lancelot, le Chevalier de la Charrette (Lancelot, the Knight of the Cart)*, written by Chrétien de Troyes – portrayed him as the most formidable of Arthur's knights. When Guinevere is abducted by Meleagant, Lancelot joins Gawain, in a quest to rescue her. In his haste, Lancelot rides two horses until they collapse and die, then encounters a cart-driving dwarf, who promises to help the knight continue his pursuit only if Lancelot rides in his cart. Humiliated, Lancelot climbs in, and after several trials along the way, arrives at the castle of Gorre. Guinevere is at first cold to Lancelot, but later, after he breaks into her tower, they spend a passionate night together.

Lancelot, whose hand was cut while climbing the tower, leaves blood on Guinevere's sheets as he sneaks out just before sunrise. Meleagant discovers the stain and accuses Guinevere of a tryst with another wounded knight, which leads to a duel with Lancelot in defense of her honor.

In later versions, Lancelot is the son of King Ban, driven from his kingdom of Benwick while Lancelot was an infant. Wounded while fleeing, Ban is being tended to by his wife when Niniane, the Lady of the Lake, absconds with the baby Lancelot. She raises the child, earning him the surname du lac, meaning "of the lake." But Niniane keeps his true family – and name – secret. Grown to adulthood, Lancelot is sent by the Lady of the Lake to Camelot, where he is a paragon of courtly behavior, compelling all who cross paths with him to remark on his perfection.

His reputation as the White Knight is built in early adventures, one of which pits him against the Dolorous Garde, a formidable castle ruled by demons and an evil Copper Knight. In the surrounding villages, the people were under its spell, suffering day and night, and unable to escape. Carrying a shield enchanted by the Lady of the Lake, the White Knight defeated twenty knights and expelled the Copper Knight from the castle, which he made his new home, the Joyous Garde. He is later led by the townspeople to a small cemetery in the castle courtyard, where he is shown an ornate tomb made of silver and gold, with a large metal slab blocking the entrance. The inscription on the slab states that it can be lifted by only one knight and that knight's name will be found beneath it. Summoning all of his strength, he lifts it over his head and sees his name: Lancelot.

Once he arrives at King Arthur's court, Lancelot falls in love with Guinevere and strives so hard to be worthy of her that she finally grants him a chaperoned assignation - and a kiss. Later, when Guinevere is kidnapped by another admirer, Lancelot crosses a bridge made from a sword, fights two lions, and defeats her abductor. Incredibly, his reward on that occasion is not thanks but scorn, because he had hesitated briefly in one small test of devotion. The lovers soon reconcile, however, and resume the relationship that eventually brings about the ruin of the Round Table.

The romance between Lancelot and Guinevere was probably inspired by another Celtic legend, told in popular twelfth-century French medieval poetry, about Tristan and Iseult. The tale is best known today through Richard Wagner's opera *Tristan und Isolde*, first produced in 1865.

Tristan was the nephew of King Mark of Cornwall, as well as the king's favorite knight. After avenging the death of his father, Tristan learns that his uncle's kingdom is being terrorized by a powerful

Irish duke named Morholt. Tristan fatally injures Morholt in combat but is wounded by his enemy's poison-smeared blade. The dying Morholt tells Tristan that only his sister, Queen Isolde, can heal the wound. Disguising himself as a harpist, Tristan plays so beautifully for the queen that she heals him so he can teach her to play the instrument. While recovering at her castle, Tristan takes notice of the Queen's daughter, the fair-skinned, golden-haired Iseult.

Returning to Cornwall, Tristan describes her beauty to his uncle, the king. A bird flying past, carrying in its beak a single strand of golden hair, causes King Mark to remark that he would only marry a woman whose hair matched it. Though their kingdoms are rivals, Tristan determines to win Iseult's hand for his uncle and returns to Ireland, which is at odds with a dragon. Iseult's father offers her as a prize to whichever knight can slay the dragon. The dragon slain, Tristan reveals both his true identity and his intentions, to broker a marriage between Iseult and King Mark, whose children would reign over all of Ireland and Cornwall. Before Iseult leaves with Tristan, her mother gives her a love potion, which she is to drink with her new husband. But during the journey, Iseult instead shares it with Tristan, causing the two to fall instantly in love. Though the princess marries King Mark, Iseult and Tristan cannot control their passion for one another. Their adultery is eventually discovered by the king, who sets a trap for the lovers. In one version of the story, Tristan is killed by a poisoned lance while playing the harp for Iseult; swooning over his body, she dies from grief.

In later versions of the Lancelot and Guinevere romance, the two are manipulated into the affair, usually by the sorceress Morgan le Fay or the Lady of the Lake. But in most, there is no love potion; the two enter willingly into their relationship. This raises a problem with Lancelot's image as perfect and saintly. Yet, like Tristan and Iseult, Lancelot and Guinevere are acquitted of their misdeeds on the basis of courtly love – a passion discovered outside of marriage that emphasizes chivalry and nobility. Even so, the legends often infer that it was his affair with Guinevere that relegated Lancelot as a footnote in the greatest of all quests undertaken by Arthur's Knights of the Round Table.

* * *

The quest for Arthur of Britain can never destroy the beauty of the works his legend has inspired or the fascination of the legend itself. Since Arthur's nobility and valor first inspired the hearts of his followers, his story has dignified the human spirit. The search for the man has become a continuing quest for what lies hidden in the hearts of all men, and it may lead us one day to the truth about the Once and Future King.

Made in the USA
Middletown, DE
14 January 2019